The Role of the Priest in Christian Initiation

With a foreword by
Cardinal Blase J. Cupich

Stephen S. Wilbricht, CSC

Nihil Obstat
Very Reverend Daniel A. Smilanic, JCD
Vicar for Canonical Services
Archdiocese of Chicago
December 27, 2016

Imprimatur
Very Reverend Ronald A. Hicks
Vicar General
Archdiocese of Chicago
December 27, 2016

The *Nihil Obstat* and *Imprimatur* are declarations that the material is free from doctrinal or moral error, and thus is granted permission to publish in accordance with c. 827. No legal responsibility is assumed by the grant of this permission. No implication is contained herein that those who have granted the *Nihil Obstat* and *Imprimatur* agree with the content, opinions, or statements expressed.

This book was edited by Mary Fox. Michael A. Dodd was the production editor, Juan Castillo was the designer, and Luis Leal was the production artist.

21 20 19 18 17 1 2 3 4 5

Printed in the United States of America.

Library of Congress Control Number: 2017932948

ISBN 978-1-61671-344-7

RPCI

For Sister Catherine Dooley, OP,

whose love and passion for liturgical catechesis

continues to echo in the hearts of her

devoted students.

Contents

Foreword

One of the joys of every priest and bishop is to celebrate the sacraments of initiation at the Easter Vigil. The Baptism, Confirmation, and celebration of the Eucharist powerfully manifest the presence of the Holy Spirit at work in the Church. The initiation of new Christians is also a witness to the work of the Church and her ministers who evangelize, catechize, and lead men and women along the path of conversion to Christ. There's no greater sign of the Church's vitality and mission than what we do at the Easter Vigil each year.

The Role of the Priest in Christian Initiation will help parishes as they seek to bring people to Christ. As the title of the book indicates, this work is specifically for priests, who have a vital role in the initiation process. Author Stephen S. Wilbricht, CSC, shows how the priest collaborates with others in the parish, bringing out their charisms to evangelize.

Fr. Wilbricht views the pastor as the one who stirs up the parish to heal, transform, and evangelize just as Christ stirred up the waters in the Pool of Bethesda to cure the ill. Jesus asked the man who had been ill, "Do you want to be well?" Our parishes have a mission to bring the joy of the Gospel to their communities. In words, actions, and attitudes, disciples today make the presence of Christ and God's mercy known to those they meet.

The pastor's role in initiation, as Fr. Wilbricht points out, is indispensable. He spreads the fervor for evangelization not only through collaboration with the initiation team but also through his preaching and his spirit of hospitality. The stranger who is greeted at the parish by a joyful pastor will want to return. It is true also that the joy of the pastor will spread to parishioners who will welcome others.

Most importantly, the priest leads people in prayer. As early as the Period of Evangelization and the Precatechumenate, he may bless and anoint the inquirers. He will preside at the Rite of Acceptance into the Order of Catechumens, the scrutinies, the Presentations of the Creed and the Lord's Prayer, and finally, he will baptize, confirm, and offer the Eucharist to those who have come to the table of the Lord. Fr. Wilbricht correctly asserts that to preside at these rites well, the priest needs to appreciate their structure and their theological meaning. The author spends much of this work, then, considering the primary symbols of the rites as well as their gestures and movements.

I hope that priests will take this insightful book to heart and realize the breadth of their ministry in Christian initiation. God calls them to journey with their parish in evangelization and with all who seek Christ. Their attention to words, gestures, sights, and sounds will bring people to contemplate Christ. That is our work.

Cardinal Blase J. Cupich
Archbishop of Chicago

Introduction

> Now there is in Jerusalem at the Sheep [Gate] a pool called in Hebrew Bethesda, with five porticoes. In these lay a large number of ill, blind, lame, and crippled. One man was there who had been ill for thirty-eight years. When Jesus saw him lying there and knew that he had been ill for a long time, he said to him, "Do you want to be well?" The sick man answered him, "Sir, I have no one to put me into the pool when the water is stirred up; while I am on my way, someone else gets down there before me." Jesus said to him, "Rise, take up your mat, and walk." Immediately the man became well, took up his mat, and walked.[1]

This sick man, whom Jesus encounters alongside the pool of healing water, was certainly not intending to become a disciple the day he was cured of his affliction. Yet, we might hope that he ran off in his elation, unable to contain the news of his restoration to health. Indeed, the call to become a follower of Jesus can take place at the most uncertain times. The sick man's life would never have changed if Jesus had not asked the simple question: "Do you want to be well?" Similarly, evangelization does not occur without announcing the Kingdom of God. The Church must be about stirring up the waters that heal and that draw new followers to Christ.

Making disciples is difficult and demanding work. When Jesus left his Apostles the command "Go, therefore, and make disciples of all the nations, baptizing them in the name of the Father, and of the Son, and of the holy Spirit,"[2] he was bestowing upon them a gargantuan task. Calling men and women into the Lord's service

1. John 5:2–9.
2. Matthew 28:19.

takes conviction and courage. The Acts of the Apostles opens with Peter addressing a great crowd, calling for their repentance and their Baptism; from this crowd "about three thousand persons were added that day."[3] Making disciples is exciting and life-giving, as joining members to Christ inspires hope in every age.

Forming Christians is the work of the entire Church, clergy and laity alike. The "General Introduction," which guides and governs Christian initiation, states: "The preparation for baptism and Christian instruction are both of vital concern to God's people, the Church, which hands on and nourishes the faith received from the apostles."[4] All of the baptized share in the responsibility of evangelization, of proclaiming Christ and the Kingdom of God by both their spoken word and their lived example. "Therefore it is most important that catechists and other laypersons should work with priests and deacons in the preparation for baptism."[5]

The work of Christian initiation offers the Church the challenge to see itself like divine life itself, as "ever ancient, ever new."[6] Walking with those who are coming to know Jesus for the first time is a humbling privilege that calls those who long ago entered the waters of Baptism to accept the call of ongoing conversion. Baptism is a daily obligation that requires renewal and reinvigoration. Baptism is the sacrament by which we respond to the summons of the Gospel; it is the means by which we discover our identity as the Church. The work of Christian initiation keeps alive the image of the Church as a people on a pilgrim journey, the journey of faith, the journey that leads to the Kingdom of God.

Stirring Up the Waters

The *Rite of Christian Initiation of Adults* is the blueprint by which the Church celebrates initiation as a ritual process. All cultures have rites of passage that celebrate meaningful milestones in individuals' lives. The Catholic Church has such rites of passage in its initiation process —a process that takes an extensive period of time and is marked by

3. Acts 2:41.

4. *Christian Initiation*, General Introduction (CI), 7.

5. CI, 7.

6. Augustine, *The Confessions* (Lib. 7, 10, 18; 10, 27: CSEL 33, 157–163. 255).

graduated steps. One does not simply present himself or herself for Baptism without considerable exposure to the Gospel and hours spent immersed in the life of the community. Those coming to Christ are invited to enter into an apprenticeship, whereby the fullness of life in Christ is revealed through gradual immersion into the mysteries of faith.

By his preaching, the priest stirs up the assembly to evangelize.

While bishops are "the chief stewards of the mysteries of God and leaders of the entire liturgical life" in their dioceses,[7] and therefore have oversight over initiation, parish priests are generally those most responsible for baptismal formation and the celebration of initiatory rituals. Because the *Rite of Christian Initiation of Adults* highlights the intrinsic relationship between preaching the Word and celebrating with a liturgical response, the priest, who makes preaching and sacramental celebration the center of his ministry, ought to have a certain intuition regarding the process of initiation in general. The participation of the parish priest in Christian formation is thus indispensable. In a very real sense, it is the pastor who has the primary role of "stirring up the waters": of evangelizing and preaching with passion, of summoning the parish community to make initiation its work, of organizing and supporting a team of catechists and teachers, and of journeying with all those on the road to Baptism and fullness of life in Christ.

This book examines the overall vision of the *Rite of Christian Initiation of Adults* as it provides opportunities for participation by the pastor and other parish priests. It presumes that the direction of Christian formation resides in the office of pastor but is shared with lay catechists who provide most of the instruction for the unbaptized and the organization of the catechumenate in general. For the busy pastor, who has untold pressures and daily distractions, this book seeks to stimulate reflection on the questions: "What can I do to be a good shepherd for my flock? How can I stir up life-giving waters for all of God's people?"

7. CI, 12.

Chapter 1

The Vision of the Rite of Christian Initiation of Adults

In the *Constitution on the Sacred Liturgy*, the Fathers of the Second Vatican Council prescribed that the rite of Baptism of adults be revised and an adult catechumenate restored.[1] Subsequently, the Congregation for Divine Worship worked with the Consilium, which had been authorized for the implementation of the *Constitution on the Sacred Liturgy*, to prepare a new rite for the Christian initiation of adults. Pope Paul VI promulgated that rite in 1972. Its first English translation, prepared by the International Commission on English in the Liturgy (ICEL), was issued in 1974 and published again in 1988 with various emendations. This version incorporates the *National Statutes for the Catechumenate*, which the National Conference of Catholic Bishops approved in November 1986.

The English translation of the *editio typica* of the *Rite of Christian Initiation of Adults* is 375 pages. It contains an overall vision for initiation and should be read as one entire and continuous itinerary for Christian formation. While some may think of the book as containing various rites for initiation, each distinct part is inseparable from the whole. The "periods" and the "steps" that constitute the structure are the rite itself. Just as the Triduum is envisioned as

1. *Constitution on the Sacred Liturgy*, 64–66.

one continuous liturgy that spans from the Evening Mass of the Lord's Supper on Holy Thursday through the celebration of Evening Prayer on Easter Sunday, so the *Rite of Christian Initiation of Adults* is to be seen as one continuous celebration of conversion from the first moments of inquiry through the Period of Mystagogy. Christian initiation is to be viewed holistically, with God's mysterious intervention acting continuously throughout.

The opening paragraphs from *Christian Initiation*, "General Introduction," provide various reasons for the Church's need to order sacraments for the making of disciples. Quite simply these reasons are: freedom from sin so as to participate in the Paschal Mystery; incorporation into the Body of Christ, the Church; and mission in the word "so that the whole human race may be brought into the unity of God's family."[2] Here we have the vision for what constitutes the sacraments of initiation. "Thus the three sacraments of Christian initiation closely combine to bring us, the faithful of Christ, to his full stature and to enable us to carry out the mission of the entire people of God in the Church and in the world."[3]

The "General Introduction" continues to expand on the dignity of Baptism, which is "the door to life and to the kingdom of God."[4] Baptism "is a sacramental bond of unity linking all who have been signed by it,"[5] and is thus a sacramental social-leveler that casts the mighty from their thrones and lifts up the lowly (see Luke 1:52). The "General Introduction" testifies that Baptism "washes away every stain of sin, original and personal";[6] however, this washing is not a private remedy but the means by which one is brought into the household of God in Christ Jesus. Echoing the Apostle Paul, the "General Introduction" states:

2. CI, 2.
3. CI, 2.
4. CI, 3.
5. CI, 4.
6. CI, 5.

> Those who are baptized are united to Christ in a death like his; buried with him in death, they are given life again with him, and with him they rise again. For baptism recalls and makes present the paschal mystery itself, because in baptism we pass from the death of sin into life.[7]

While the Baptism of either infants or adults recognizes the work of God refashioning his creation into his "adopted children"[8] in Christ, the initiation of adults has particular power to make present for the Church the death of the old self so as to rise in the person of Christ. This is perhaps the greatest gift the restored catechumenate has bestowed upon the Church.

A Brief Historical Snapshot of Initiation

What is today called the catechumenate has its roots in the early Church, when it was dangerous to be a Christian. While the Acts of the Apostles describes a Christian community that was publicly visible,[9] a century had not passed before the Church found itself in hiding and needing to protect itself from those desiring to infiltrate its boundaries with the intention to destroy. Thus, Justin Martyr provides witness around the year 150 of an "apology" designed to explain to outsiders, whose trustworthiness had been carefully tested, the meaning behind such mysteries as the Eucharist.[10]

The work, sketchily attributed to Hippolytus of Rome and written possibly in the early third century, served most useful in the restoration of the catechumenate.[11] The *Apostolic Tradition* outlines a three-year plan for formation that includes prayer and regular laying on of hands as well as the expectation that catechumens would engage in works of charity. It furthermore places great emphasis upon the scrutinizing of candidates for Baptism and suggests a genuine belief in turning away from the allurements of the pagan world before one

---

7. CI, 6.

8. CI, 2.

9. "Every day they devoted themselves to meeting together in the temple area and to breaking bread in their homes. They ate their meals with exultation and sincerity of heart, praising God and enjoying favor with all the people. And every day the Lord added to their number those who were being saved" (Acts 2:46–47).

10. See E.C. Whitaker, *Documents of the Baptismal Liturgy* (London: SPCK, 1970), 1–2.

11. Paul Bradshaw, Maxwell E. Johnson, and L. Edward Phillips, *The Apostolic Tradition, Hermeneia: A Critical and Historical Commentary on the Bible* (Minneapolis: Fortress Press, 2002).

could become members of Christ. The association of Baptism with the Easter Vigil and the role of the bishop in performing a second postbaptismal anointing as the newly baptized were presented to him in the midst of the assembly are evidenced in the instructions provided in the *Apostolic Tradition.*

By the late fourth century, as the Church had emerged from hiding and had taken up an influential position in the Roman Empire, both East and West, the works of several influential bishops give witness to the power of mystagogical preaching. Cyril of Jerusalem (†387), Ambrose of Milan (†397), John Chrysostom of Constantinople (†407), Theodore of Mopsuestia (†428), and Augustine of Hippo (†430), each in his unique style and location, provide insights into the rites that are incorporated into today's adult catechumenate. Some of these rites include the submission of names to the bishop for election, the scrutinies on the Third, Fourth, and Fifth Sundays of Lent, the Presentation of the Creed to be "returned" in recited form later, and the Presentation of the Lord's Prayer. The homilies delivered to catechumens and neophytes by these great preachers suggest a period of embellishment in the catechumenate with a need for ritual expression that captures the seriousness of the conversion of those coming into the Church.

It did not take long for the Church to become fully ensconced in the cultures of the Roman West and the Byzantine East, thereby establishing the beginnings of Christendom. By the Middle Ages, the adult catechumenate had largely fallen out of use, as infant Baptism became normative. Nevertheless, the ritual books that were disseminated around the empire continued to contain prayers for catechumens. For example, the revered *Gelasian Sacramentary*, from the seventh century, includes formularies for Scrutiny Masses and for Masses for the Presentation of the Creed and the Lord's Prayer.[12] However, by the tenth century, Roman pontificals began to include a condensed rite in which all of the prebaptismal ceremonies could take place in a single ritual.[13] As infant Baptism became more and more the common form of initiation, the need for an extended process of prebaptismal formation and ritual celebration began to

12. Paul Turner, *The Hallelujah Highway: A History of the Catechumenate* (Chicago: Liturgy Training Publications, 2000), 95.

13. Turner, 106.

fall into the background of the Christian imagination. Baptism became something done to a baby rather than what marked the life choice of committed discipleship on the part of a grown adult.

Yet the vision of adult initiation was never quite suppressed in the Church. The 1614 *Roman Ritual*, compiled after the theological controversies of the Reformation era and the Council of Trent, continues to put forth an extended rite for adults alongside a condensed version for infants.[14] At this very time, however, missionaries were traveling the globe seeking to convert cultures en masse to Christianity. Their labors to engage peoples who had never heard of Christ challenged the Church to consider the value of ritualizing conversion as a passage in stages.[15] It would take several centuries for the Church to embrace a return to initiation based on developmental progress that is measured in periods of time and is celebrated accordingly.

Religious Conversion as Journey

The vision of adult formation based on the gradual development of a life of faith is contained in the opening paragraph of the "Introduction" to the *Rite of Christian Initiation of Adults*. It suggests that adults must have the opportunity first to "hear" the Word of God, second to come to a personal decision to "freely seek" after God, and third to enter the "way of faith":

> The rite of Christian initiation presented here is designed for adults who, after hearing the mystery of Christ proclaimed, consciously and freely seek the living God and enter the way of faith and conversion as the Holy Spirit opens their hearts. By God's help they will be strengthened spiritually during their preparation and at the proper time will receive the sacraments fruitfully.[16]

The words "consciously" and "freely" in this passage underscore the nature of the adult commitment to Christ: it is one made as a result of journeying with him and witnessing his action in the world. It is unfortunate that the Christian initiation process is understood by many to be an institutionalized *program* that too often is modeled

14. Turner, 138.

15. Turner, 140.

16. *Rite of Christian Initiation of Adults* (RCIA), 1.

Adults must have the opportunity to hear the Word of God, decide to freely seek God, and enter the way of faith.

after our education system of imparting and digesting classroom information rather than as a life *process* that unfolds in mysterious, non-calculable ways.

The seventh chapter of *Lumen gentium* is entitled "The Pilgrim Church." It defines the nature of the Church as the "communion of the whole mystical body of Jesus Christ"[17] in which the members on earth are making a pilgrim journey to the oneness that is full participation in divine life. Christian life is a pilgrimage of journeying each day with an openness to seeing God's desire to unite all things:

> When the Lord will come in glory, and all his angels with him (see Mt 25:31), death will be no more and all things will be subject to him (see 1 Cor 15:26–27). But at the present time some of his disciples are pilgrims on earth, others have died and are being purified, while still others are in glory, contemplating "in full light, God himself triune and one, exactly as he is." All of us, however, in varying degrees and in different ways share in the same love of God and our neighbor, and we all sing the same hymn of glory to our God. All, indeed, who are of Christ and who have his Spirit form one church and in Christ are joined together (Eph 4:16).[18]

To be a pilgrim, however, one must be dedicated. A pilgrim is attentive and aware. The willingness to journey through life without clinging to the comfortable and the well known but with a delight in encountering hardships and embracing sacrifices separates a pilgrim from a tourist. A pilgrim Church is one that resists being too

17. *Lumen gentium* (LG), 50.

18. LG, 49.

anchored in one place but is daily challenged to transcend itself and to launch itself into the mystery of the horizon. Pilgrimage is a way of life demanding an attitude of surrender.

A pilgrim people approaches the world not from the perspective of strict order and control but from a desire to be attentive and alert to what the surprises along the way can teach. Thus, heartfelt and mature discernment is a keystone of the *Rite of Christian Initiation of Adults*. The Introduction to the RCIA describes this necessary discernment as taking place within the "community of the faithful":

> The initiation of catechumens is a gradual process that takes place within the community of the faithful. By joining the catechumens in reflecting on the value of the paschal mystery and by renewing their own conversion, the faithful provide an example that will help the catechumens to obey the Holy Spirit more generously.
>
> The rite of initiation is suited to a spiritual journey of adults that varies according to the many forms of God's grace, the free cooperation of the individuals, the action of the Church, and the circumstances of time and place.[19]

Once again, a pilgrim way of life is the hallmark of Christianity and is the goal to which seekers attend. How do adults cooperate with the "many forms of God's grace"? How does the Church walk with them in such a way so as to raise questions about the working of God at every turn in the road? The "free cooperation" of participants is crucial, as the initiation process resists the mass production of "cookie-cutter" disciples. At times, inquirers and catechumens will resist responding to God's voice and the invitation to do his will. The Church is invited to respond with patience.

Some would suggest that conversion entails a 180-degree turn in life, whereby former allegiances and attractions are completely shed. Conversion is thereby envisioned as a work largely determined by the effort of the one seeking it. The question is whether conversion is our doing or the work of God that we gradually discover and in which we are gradually re-created. St. Augustine in fifth-century Africa reminded the newly converted of his church:

19. RCIA, 4–5.

> Remember, you did not exist, and you were created: you were carried to the Lord's threshing floor. . . . [W]hen you were set aside as catechumens you were stored in his barn. You gave in your names: you began to be ground with fasting and exorcism. After that you came to water, were moistened and made one. You were cooked then, when the ardour of the Holy Spirit came near, and now have been made the Lord's bread.[20]

Augustine suggests that conversion is not so much an act of the will as it is a willingness to be "carried" and even "cooked." He makes the point that conversion cannot be forced. It involves coming to terms with a growing awareness that life is not what it used to be, that relationships have changed, and that previous life goals no longer dictate decisions.

A helpful way of conceiving of conversion as a process is by understanding it as the "successful negation of crisis."[21] Every human life will involve crises, some highly dramatic and others agonizingly private, all of which are beyond one's choosing. One does not choose crisis. In fact, it is human nature to deny crisis and to avoid it at all costs. We are more comfortable with life as we know it rather than accepting what is beyond our control. In the case of Christian initiation and the call to conversion, moments of crisis can be as seemingly simple as the joy of a child's birth or the sadness of a parent's death. The world changes as relationships shift, and how one responds to crisis affects the journey of conversion. The late theologian Mark Searle suggests, for example, that the turning point of conversion is the moment of surrender to the truth of one's life (something that most people are afraid to do on a regular basis). He writes:

> It may not be a sudden and dramatic event; one may not be able to pinpoint the moment of its coming or to say quite where or when or how it happened. Yet in some mysterious way one is aware that something new has been born. A new life has begun to quicken, a quiet joy, deep-seated and intangible, and a more deeply rooted peace begin to make themselves felt beneath and beyond the continuing darkness and disorder. Order is not at once restored, still less is the old order reestablished: to that there can be no going back. Yet gradually one is led to a new set of relationships, more genuine and more realistic, with one's world. The

20. Whitaker, *Documents of the Baptismal Liturgy*, 160.

21. Mark Searle, "The Journey of Conversion," *Worship* 54, no. 1 (1980): 36.

> sense of futile restlessness gives way perhaps to a growing sense of new direction and meaningfulness. One's defeats and failures are not taken away, but forgiven. Physical and material losses are not necessarily made good, but perhaps the sense of loss is transformed into that detachment which is the condition for genuine freedom.[22]

Conversion for those coming to the Christian faith might be summed up as a genuine living of Christ's Paschal Mystery. The shift in life that Searle describes is death to one way of looking at the world in order to see it in a new light. The Suffering, Death, and Resurrection of Christ are to be the framework into which the Christian paints the portrait of life. "The whole initiation must bear a markedly paschal character, since the initiation of Christians is the first sacramental sharing in Christ's dying and rising."[23]

One of the great gifts that the Christian initiation process gives the Church is the impression it makes upon the Christian community that the journey of conversion is the work of the entire community. The *Rite of Christian Initiation of Adults* calls for the participation of every member of Christ's Body, in prayer for future disciples, in sacramental celebration, in teaching, and in performing works of charity.

The RCIA states:

> The people of God, as represented by the local Church, should understand and show by their concern that the initiation of adults is the responsibility of all the baptized. Therefore the community must always be fully prepared in the pursuit of its apostolic vocation to give help to those who are searching for Christ. In the various circumstances of daily life, even as in the apostolate, all the followers of Christ have the obligation of spreading the faith according to their abilities.[24]

22. Ibid., 42.
23. RCIA, 8.
24. RCIA, 9.

Through their participation in the liturgy, their signs of welcome, and their examples of renewal, the whole parish takes part in the Christian initiation process.

The rite continues by concretely describing the work of the faithful in the process of conversion: "They should therefore show themselves ready to give the candidates evidence of the spirit of the Christian community and to welcome them into their homes, into personal conversation, and into community gatherings";[25] They should be present for liturgical celebrations and "should take an active part in the responses, prayers, singing and acclamations";[26] "On the day of election, because it is a day of growth for the community, the faithful, when called upon, should be sure to give honest and carefully considered testimony about the catechumens."[27] They should "take care to participate in the rites of the scrutinies and presentations and give the elect the example of their own renewal in the spirit of penance, faith, and charity."[28] "At the Easter Vigil, they should attach great importance to renewing their own baptismal promises."[29]

25. RCIA, 9 §1.
26. RCIA, 9 §2.
27. RCIA, 9 §3.
28. RCIA, 9 §4.
29. RCIA, 9 §4.

Finally, the rite states, "During the period immediately after baptism, the faithful should take part in the Masses for neophytes, that is, the Sunday Masses of the Easter season, welcome the neophytes with open arms in charity, and help them to feel more at home in the community of the baptized."[30]

If taken seriously, this is a tall agenda for the Christian community. Making disciples is hard work. Nevertheless, participation by the entire community in the process of Christian initiation reveals that living as pilgrims demands cooperating with and growing from the experiences of others. Along the pilgrim way of life, a person stumbles and falls; others are there to pick him up and to help her begin anew. There are days on the journey of life when tempers flare and relationships are threatened; the pilgrim surrenders pride and ego and is willing to reconcile. On some dark days, the Christian way seems like a foolish waste of time; it is the work of a Church that is constantly renewing herself and is aware of her ongoing transformation to instill a hope that counters despair.

Following a "Pilgrim" Schedule

Continuing with the image of the Church as a pilgrim people, the *Rite of Christian Initiation of Adults* directs that the movement of the Spirit is to be followed rather than a set time period. Religious conversion does not unfold according to a timetable. Therefore, the Christian initiation process tries to make readiness the measure by which candidates progress along the way to full maturity in Christ. The rite attempts to mark this progress by a series of "periods" and "steps" that indicate spiritual advancement: "This journey includes not only the periods for making inquiry and for maturing, but also the steps marking the catechumens' progress, as they pass, so to speak, through another doorway or ascend to the next level."[31] Even though a schedule may be developed for the four periods and three steps of the rite, this schedule must always be considered fluid—adaptable to the individual needs of the seekers, the catechumens, the elect, and the neophytes.

---

30. RCIA, 9 §5.

31. RCIA, 6.

It is most appropriate, therefore, for the parish to have a year-round precatechumenate as well as a year-round catechumenate. This means that the local church, in keeping with its fundamental ministry of evangelization, will welcome men and women into the process of conversion at any point in the calendar year. If someone were to step forward in January with a desire to discover the Christian faith, it does not serve them well to be told to wait for the start of the precatechumenate in September. For this reason, the *National Statutes for the Catechumenate* prescribes that the precatechumenate be informal:

> Any reception or service of welcome or prayer for inquirers at the beginning or during a precatechumenate (or in an earlier period of evangelization) must be entirely informal. Such meetings should take into account that the inquirers are not yet catechumens and that the rite of acceptance into the order of catechumens, intended for those who have been converted from unbelief and have initial faith, may not be anticipated.[32]

The informality of the precatechumenate suggests that there should be no definitive moment when the period of inquiry begins; it is regular and ongoing. Keeping this vision alive requires greater work on the part of the Christian initiation team, as it reveals discernment, not the calendar, as the tool to determine readiness for the Rite of Acceptance into the Order of Catechumens.

Similarly, while the catechumenate is necessarily more formally structured, it too is to resist following the precise timeline of the calendar. The *National Statutes for the Catechumenate* suggests that "a thoroughly comprehensive catechesis on the truths of Catholic doctrine and moral life, aided by approved catechetical texts, is to be provided during the period of the catechumenate (see RCIA, no. 75)." [33] The words *thoroughly comprehensive* are significant here. One must ask: what does "thoroughly comprehensive" mean? For some along the way to Christ, a "thoroughly comprehensive" catechesis might take place in a year's time, while for some (like St. Augustine) it could take many years to discern readiness for election. The *National Statutes* demand a catechumenate of "at least" one year:

---

32. *National Statutes for the Catechumenate* (NS), 1.

33. NS, 7.

> The period of the catechumenate, beginning at acceptance into the order of catechumens and including both the catechumenate proper and the period of purification and enlightenment after election or enrollment of names, should extend for at least one year of formation, instruction, and probation. Ordinarily this period should go from at least the Easter season of one year until the next; preferably it should begin before Lent in one year and extend until Easter of the following year.[34]

While the mandate for a yearlong catechumenate is normative in the United States, the bishops understand that exceptions to this rule may indeed apply according to individual circumstances. They allow, therefore, for an "abbreviated catechumenate," which the diocesan bishop "may permit only in individual and exceptional cases."[35] The rite states: "The extraordinary circumstances in question are either events that prevent the candidate from completing all the steps of the catechumenate or a depth of Christian conversion and a degree of religious maturity that lead the local bishop to decide that the candidate may receive baptism without delay."[36] The next paragraph in the rite further expands upon the nature of these "extraordinary circumstances": "Sickness, old age, change of residence, long absence for travel, may sometimes either prevent a candidate from celebrating the rite of acceptance that leads to the period of the catechumenate or, having begun the catechumenate, from completing it by participation in all the rites belonging to the period."[37] Because the determination to abbreviate the catechumenate requires the approval of the local bishop, this option must be considered truly "exceptional."

In sum, the basic vision of the *Rite of Christian Initiation of Adults* is based on the mystery of the working of grace in the life of the Christian community. The outpouring of the Holy Spirit is not dictated by the passing of days or the changing of seasons but according to God's abundant mercy. Adult initiation attempts to be attentive to this generous gift. As pilgrims on a journey, the Church as a whole discovers itself to be a community in need of daily conversion.

34. NS, 6.

35. NS, 20.

36. RCIA, 331.

37. RCIA, 332.

Chapter 2

The Role of the Priest in Christian Initiation

One of the primary assumptions of this book is that pastors are busy. Whether they oversee large inner-city parishes, struggling to sustain communal vitality and economic viability, or whether they serve in remote parts of their diocese, caring for more than one worshipping community, pastors (including assistant parish priests) almost universally experience a sense of being stretched to the limits. With the obligation to fulfill a number of roles, from the presider at the sacraments—in such diverse moments as the joy of Baptism and the sadness of illness and death—to acting as the chief financial officer of the parish, to managing a professional ministerial staff, priests are expected to function each day wearing a variety of hats.

Gone are the days when priests could focus the majority of their attention on the duties of preaching the Gospel, celebrating the sacraments, visiting the sick, and fulfilling the daily obligation of praying their breviary. Among all their tasks, priests bear the overall responsibility for building up the Christian community by actively working to establish and renew relationship among God's people. As the Second Vatican Council decree on the ministry and life of priests, *Presbyterorum ordinis*, states:

> The pastor's task is not limited to individual care of the faithful. It extends by right also to the formation of a genuine Christian community. But a

> properly cultivated community spirit must embrace not only the local church but the universal church. A local community ought not merely to promote the care of its own faithful, but should be imbued with the missionary spirit and should smooth the path to Christ for all people. But it must regard as its special charge those under instruction and the newly converted who are being gradually formed to know and live the christian life.[1]

These words leave no doubt that a pastor's time and energy is not only taken up with caring for the parish and its daily spiritual and temporal needs but is also to be spent embracing the work of the universal Church—in particular, evangelizing those who have yet to hear the voice of Christ and who are on the initial road to conversion. Attending to the flock's pastoral care, while simultaneously looking to the world beyond, is daunting for even the most seasoned shepherd.

Setting the Tone for Initiation

In the midst of his busy schedule, the parish priest might very well pose the question to himself: "What should I do to best be involved in the ministry of initiation?" The first way he may answer this question is by his very attitude toward initiation. How dedicated is the priest to the project of evangelization? Pope Paul VI, in his 1975 apostolic exhortation *Evangelii nuntiandi*, writes: "What identifies our priestly service, gives a profound unity to the thousand and one tasks which claim our attention day by day and throughout our lives, and confers a distinct character on our activities, is this aim, ever present in all our action: to proclaim the Gospel of God."[2] Pope John Paul II further underscores the priest's renewed effort in the work of evangelization in his 1992 apostolic exhortation *Pastores dabo vobis*:

> Today, in particular, the pressing pastoral task of the new evangelization calls for the involvement of the entire People of God, and requires a new fervor, new methods and a new expression for announcing and witnessing of the Gospel. This task demands priests who are deeply and fully immersed in the mystery of Christ and capable of embodying a new style of pastoral life, marked by a profound communion with the pope, the bishops and other priests, and a fruitful cooperation with the lay

1. *Presbyterorum ordinis*, 6.
2. *Evangelii nuntiandi* (EN), 68.

> faithful, always respecting and fostering the different roles, charisms and ministries present within the ecclesial community.[3]

The pastor's desire to respect and foster the dynamic charisms within the Body of Christ shows his interest in evangelization.

Undoubtedly, the pastor proclaims the Gospel in a myriad of ways throughout the day, but how do acts of evangelization reveal a conviction that inviting men and women to discipleship is the cornerstone of the parish itself? A true mark of promoting evangelization is the pastor's authentic desire to respect and foster the dynamic charisms within the Body of Christ. His desire is such because the Gospel is best manifested when each part of Christ's Body is enabled to offer itself for the good of the whole.

Christian Initiation, "General Introduction," provides several requirements by which the priest is to demonstrate respect for the sacraments of initiation and, by extension, to the overall mission of evangelization. First, priests are to honor the fact that they are first and foremost representatives of Christ: "In every celebration of this sacrament (Baptism) they should be mindful that they act in the Church in the name of Christ and by the power of the Holy Spirit."[4] Second, pastors must be conscious of the "way" in which they approach and celebrate the sacraments: "They should therefore be diligent in the ministry of the word of God and in the manner of celebrating the sacraments."[5] A simple litmus test would be to examine the effort and the time devoted to homily preparation. Finally, pastors are asked to respect the boundaries of their parish and are not to baptize in foreign territories without permission: "Except in a case of necessity, these ministers are not to confer baptism outside their own territory, even on their own subjects,

3. *Pastores dabo vobis*, 18.
4. CI, 11 §1.
5. CI, 11 §2.

without the requisite permission."[6] These regulations serve as reminders that initiation is the work of Jesus Christ and that the priest is called to humbly participate in his ministry rather than act according to his own authority.

Just as Jesus greeted the curiosity of John's disciples with the directive "Come, and you will see,"[7] so pastors most clearly embody an evangelical spirit when they are hospitable and welcoming. Hospitable priests welcome strangers and invite them to participation. Pope Francis, in his papal bull proclaiming the Jubilee of Mercy in 2015, alludes to the joyful and hospitable attitude that is to flow from priests: "We priests have received the gift of the Holy Spirit for the forgiveness of sins, and we are responsible for this. None of us wields power over this Sacrament; rather, we are faithful servants of God's mercy through it. Every confessor must accept the faithful as the father in the parable of the prodigal son: a father who runs out to meet his son despite the fact that he has squandered away his inheritance."[8] The priest must scrutinize his demeanor and ask whether his is the joyful vulnerability of the faithful father who welcomes home his lost son. There is no denying the prophetic nature of a pastoral approach that is welcoming and hospitable.

Providing Pastoral Counseling and Aid

Beyond the priest's obligation to set the overall tone for evangelization and Christian initiation within the local community, the pastor is to serve as a primary giver of spiritual support to not only the men and women seeking to come into the Church but also those who are guiding their formation. The priest is to act as a shepherd who diligently guards the flock entrusted to him. Making himself available from the outset of the Christian initiation process is extremely valuable for the general well-being of the formation community. The Introduction to the RCIA states:

> Priests, in addition to their usual ministry for any celebration of baptism, confirmation, and the eucharist, have the responsibility of attending to the pastoral and personal care of the catechumens,

6. CI, 11 §3.
7. John 1:38–39.
8. *Misericordiae vultus* (MV), 17.

> especially those who seem hesitant and discouraged. With the help of deacons and catechists, they are to provide instruction for the catechumens; they are also to approve the choice of godparents and willingly listen to and help them; they are to be diligent in the correct celebration and adaptation of the rites throughout the entire course of Christian initiation.[9]

The pastoral responsibilities of the priest as shepherd contained in this paragraph are: (1) presiding "correctly" at the sacraments (and other rites), (2) encouraging those in need (the "hesitant" and the "discouraged"), (3) teaching the faith, and (4) involving themselves in the selection of godparents. The priest is therefore to understand the process as a whole and is to know those participating in it. A personal relationship with all those participating in the *Rite of Christian Initiation of Adults* will aid inquirers and catechumens in their discernment to progress along the way toward the sacraments of initiation.

While the pastor should make himself available at all times throughout the process of initiation, there are particular moments when he is needed to enact his role as a spiritual guide. One such moment occurs prior to the Rite of Acceptance into the Order of Catechumens. After a period of inquiry, some men and women will express the desire to hear the Gospel and to begin apprenticeship in the Christian life. Prior to being accepted into the Order of Catechumens, it is necessary for them to truly discern God's will in their lives. Pastors have the responsibility to participate in this discernment prior to acceptance. The RCIA states:

> Before the rite is celebrated, therefore, sufficient and necessary time, as required in each case, should be set aside to evaluate and, if necessary, to purify the candidates' motives and dispositions. With the help of the sponsors, catechists, and deacons, parish priests (pastors) have the responsibility for judging the outward indications of such dispositions. Because of the effect of baptism once validly received, it is the duty of parish priests (pastors) to see to it that no baptized person seeks for any reason whatever to be baptized a second time.[10]

9. RCIA, 13.
10. RCIA, 43.

Though this instruction suggests that a key responsibility of the pastor is to prevent anyone from being rebaptized, the more fundamental reason for this counseling is to help clarify motives on the part of inquirers. This is the moment for the priest to ask the basic question: What are you looking for? When the priest receives a response, it then becomes his role to help purify that intention, reminding the seeker that relationship with Christ is a matter of the heart, not established to satisfy anyone else, not to please a parent, a spouse, or a child.

Another potential moment for spiritual guidance, although not specified by the RCIA itself, is in the final days of the Period of Purification and Enlightenment leading up to the final preparation on Holy Saturday. If the process begins with the priest asking seekers, "Why have you come?" it is logical that the priest should also make an inquiry into the faith lives of the elect prior to their Baptism. At this point, the query "Why have you come?" would be followed with the additional question "Why have you stayed?" Undoubtedly, after an extensive period of catechesis and participation in liturgical formation, as well as works of charity, the reasons the elect give for the desire to be baptized will be different from the ones provided at the time of inquiry.

Providing for a Catechetical Team

The *Rite of Christian Initiation of Adults* clearly envisions that conversion requires a ministry of collaboration. It was not long ago that a non-Christian would be catechized solely by the parish priest in the confines of the rectory. There was nothing public about adult initiation. The "General Introduction" to *Christian Initiation* clearly states that initiation is the work of the community. No member of Christ's Body is excluded from the work of proclaiming the Gospel to every creature and to journeying with those who discover a new relationship with Christ:

> The preparation for baptism and Christian instruction are both of vital concern to God's people, the Church, which hands on and nourishes the faith received from the apostles. Through the ministry of the Church, adults are called to the Gospel by the Holy Spirit and infants are baptized in the faith of the Church and brought up in that faith. Therefore

> it is most important that catechists and other laypersons should work with priests and deacons in the preparation for baptism.[11]

Priests, as well as deacons, have the facility to teach the faith, but they recognize that this ministry is shared with the non-ordained. Pastors must stir up the full participation of the parish in the initiation process. Fundamentally, this means that a team of catechists, sponsors, ministers of hospitality, etc., needs to be developed and supported.

The employment of a director of Christian initiation ought to be considered a norm rather than a luxury. This individual should be formed in the vision of Christian initiation and have a thorough understanding of the periods and steps of the entire process. The *Rite of Christian Initiation of Adults* places a high value on the training and the ministerial suitability of those called to catechize on behalf of the Church:

> Catechists, who have an important office for the progress of the catechumens and for the growth of the community, should, whenever possible, have an active part in the rites. When deputed by the bishop, they may perform the minor exorcisms and blessings contained in the ritual. When they are teaching, catechists should see that their instruction is filled with the spirit of the Gospel, adapted to the liturgical signs and

To ensure high-quality catechesis, it is valuable for the pastor to participate in the discernmenet process with the Christian initiation team.

11. CI, 7.

> the cycle of the Church's year, suited to the needs of the catechumens, and as far as possible enriched by local traditions.[12]

Pastors have an obligation to ensure that the instruction men and women are given throughout the Christian initiation process is of the highest quality. This is why it is vitally important that the pastor participate in a discernment process regarding the gifts and charisms of the team members. Not all who wish to form Christians are suitable teachers, and some of the best teachers do not make good leaders of prayer. The RCIA states: "The instruction that the catechumens receive during this period (the catechumenate) should be of a kind that while presenting Catholic teaching in its entirety also enlightens faith, directs the heart toward God, fosters participation in the liturgy, inspires apostolic activity, and nurtures a life completely in accord with the spirit of Christ."[13] This mandate is best fulfilled when a team works together to draw on one another's strengths.

How might this type of collaboration unfold practically? First, it is important to designate various ministries within the Christian initiation process. For example, one person could coordinate hospitality on a regular basis, ensuring that the environment is welcoming and food and drink are provided during breaks. Another person could be designated as the prayer coordinator, making sure that opportunities for prayer are well-orchestrated. The chief catechist would have the role of guaranteeing that those instructing on a particular topic are well-suited for the task. Another person on the team might have little desire to instruct with words but is able to instruct with actions; perhaps that person could be responsible for organizing charitable projects for the catechumens and the elect. The Christian initiation process is most effective when it is led by a team of men and women who know their strengths and weaknesses and who see the work of Christian formation as the work of the entire Church.

To support the functioning of the Christian initiation team, it follows that the parish priest would want to create a budget that undergirds the initiation process. The formation of adults requires a creativity that will cost money. It is often difficult to see ministry in

12. RCIA, 16.

13. RCIA, 78.

the duty of fundraising, yet that is what it is. Henri Nouwen writes on a spirituality of fundraising:

> From the perspective of the gospel, fundraising is not a response to a crisis. Fundraising is, first and foremost, a form of ministry. It is a way of announcing our vision and inviting other people into our vision. Vision and mission are so central to the life of God's people that without vision we perish and without mission we lose our way. . . . Fundraising is proclaiming what we believe in such a way that we offer other people an opportunity to participation with us in our vision and our mission.[14]

Financially supporting the Christian initiation process is a role the pastor should not consider merely as behind-the-scenes; the more the parish knows and understands that formation requires professional training and ongoing funding, the more the community will want to step forward to assist. Fundraising helps to stir up the mission as a centerpiece of the community's life.

Just as fiscal responsibilities belong to the pastor, so does the duty of parish record keeping. The duty of keeping parish records of Baptism is carefully laid out in canon law: "The pastor of the place where the baptism is celebrated must carefully and without any delay record in the baptismal register the names of the baptized, with mention made of the minister, parents, sponsors, witnesses, if any, the place and date of the conferral of the baptism, and the date and place of birth."[15] Similarly, the Church asks that the names of those participating in the various steps of the RCIA be inscribed in record books. A name represents Christian dignity and belonging to the Body of Christ. For example, paragraph 46 of the RCIA states: "After the celebration of the rite of acceptance, the names of the catechumens are to be duly inscribed in the register of catechumens, along with the names of the sponsors and the minister and the date and place of the celebration."[16] These words imply the solemn dignity of acceptance. Similarly, pastors ought to ensure that the Book of the Elect is dignified and treated as a sacred object. Keeping good records and providing for dignified books themselves is an indication of the overall reverence devoted to the initiation process.

14. Henri J. M. Nouwen, *A Spirituality of Fundraising* (Nashville: Upper Room Books, 2010), 16.

15. *Code of Canon Law: Latin-English Edition: New English Translation (Codex Iuris Canonici* [CIC]) (Washington DC: Canon Law Society of America, 1998), c. 877.

16. RCIA, 46.

Presiding at the Rites

While it might seem only natural that the pastor would preside at the major liturgies as well as the minor exorcisms and blessings, it is important to underscore that this is a vital component of the Christian initiation process that must be done well. Therefore, from the outset of the process, the priest may wish to map out with the catechumenal team the opportunities for presiding at various rites. If he is not a member of the team, the priest may wish to attend the final portion of each session of instruction to lead the group in a final prayer and blessing. If this is not possible, perhaps he could arrange to be present every two or three weeks at either the beginning or the end of a gathering. The important point is that he be thoughtful and diligent in his responsibility to lead prayer with those beginning the Christian journey.

Another aspect of presiding concerns preaching. Understanding the intimate link between evangelization and initiation, the one responsible for preaching ought to consider how the homily, in general, is meant to call men and women to conversion and to relationship with Christ. *Presbyterorum ordinis* regards preaching as the "primary duty" of the ordained:

> The People of God are joined together primarily by the word of the living God. And rightfully they expect this from their priests. Since no one can be saved who does not first believe, priests, as co-workers with their bishops, have the primary duty of proclaiming the Gospel of God to all. In this way they fulfill the command of the Lord: "Go into the whole world and preach the Gospel to every creature" (Mk 16:15), and they establish and build up the People of God. Through the saving word the spark of faith is lit in the hearts of unbelievers, and fed in the hearts of the faithful. This is the way the congregation of faithful is started and grows, just as the Apostle describes: "Faith comes from hearing, and hearing through the word of Christ" (Rom 10:17).[17]

Particular public occasions for preaching, such as the Rite of Acceptance into the Order of Catechumens, the scrutinies, and the Easter Vigil, offer the priest the opportunity to prayerfully reflect on the movement of the Spirit in the lives of those being joined to Christ. These are also occasions when the priest might challenge the

17. PO, 4.

community as a whole to as a whole to evangelize. The bottom line is that the priest must see preaching as a valuable component of the Christian initiation process that deserves his time for preparation and demands his care in execution.

A final word on the role of presiding at the rites concerns the presider's right to make adaptations throughout the Christian initiation process as a whole. The *Rite of Christian Initiation of Adults* suggests that presiders are to execute a "full and intelligent use" of freedom to make adaptations according to the particular needs of their communities:

> Celebrants should make full and intelligent use of the freedom given to them either in *Christian Initiation*, General Introduction (no. 34) or in the rubrics of the rite itself. In many places the manner of acting or praying is intentionally left undetermined or two alternatives are offered, so that ministers, according to their prudent pastoral judgment, may accommodate the rite to the circumstances of the candidates and others who are present. In all the rites the greatest freedom is left in the invitation and instructions, and the intercessions may always be shortened, changed, or even expanded with new intentions, in order to fit the circumstances or special situation of the candidates (for example, a sad or joyful event occurring in a family) or of the others present (for example, sorrow or joy common to the parish or civic community).
>
> The minister will also adapt the texts by changing the gender and number as required.[18]

This governing principle of adaptation according to the pastoral needs of the community depends upon a solid knowledge of the Christian initiation process. For example, in order to make adaptations to the Rite of Acceptance into the Order of Catechumens, such as where to receive the candidates or how they are to receive the cross, the presider must have an appreciation for the structure of the rite itself as well as its theological meaning. Therefore, the remainder of this book is largely devoted to examining the four periods and the three steps for celebrating adult initiation. All priests who summon men and women to follow Christ should contemplate and cherish this rich gem of the Church.

18. RCIA, 35.

Periods and Steps in the Rite of Christian Initiation of Adults

	First Period	First Step	Second Period
	Period of Evangelization and Precatechumenate	Rite of Acceptance into the Order of Catechumens	Period of the Catechumenate
Time	Indefinite length	When inquirer and community discern readiness	At least a year (including Period of Purification and Enlightenment)
Name	**Inquirer**		**Catechumen**
What occurs during this period or step	Proclamation of the Gospel and Jesus Christ, leading to faith and initial conversion; introduction to the Christian community	Inquirers publicly declare their intention to become members of the Church; Church accepts them as catechumens.	Formation through catechesis, experience of the Christian way of life through familiarity with community, participation in the liturgical life of the community, and participation in the apostolic life of the Church
Rites belonging to the period	No formal rites; individual prayers and blessings may take place as appropriate.		Celebrations of the Word, Blessings, Anointings, Minor Exorcisms

Second Step	Third Period	Third Step	Fourth Period
Rite of Election	Period of Purification and Enlightenment	Celebration of Sacraments of Initiation	Period of Mystagogy
First Sunday of Lent	Lent	Easter Vigil	Easter Time; extended Mystagogy for one year
	Elect		**Neophyte**
In the name of the Church, the bishop judges readiness of catechumens for initiation and declares that they are chosen for sacraments at the next Easter Vigil.	Retreat-like preparation for the celebration of sacraments of initiation	Initiation into the Church through Baptism, Confirmation, and Eucharist	Deepening understanding of Paschal Mystery though meditation on the Gospel, participation in the Eucharist, and doing works of charity
	Scrutinies, Presentations of the Creed and Lord's Prayer, Preparatory Rites on Holy Saturday		Sunday Masses of Easter Time; celebrations near Pentecost and anniversary of initiation; Mass with the bishop

Chapter 3

First Period / First Step: Inquiry and Acceptance

> As he passed by the Sea of Galilee, he saw Simon and his brother Andrew casting their nets into the sea; they were fishermen. Jesus said to them, "Come after me, and I will make you fishers of men." Then they abandoned their nets and followed him. He walked along a little farther and saw James, the son of Zebedee, and his brother John. They too were in a boat mending their nets. Then he called them. So they left their father Zebedee in the boat along with the hired men and followed him.[1]

The Gospel according to Mark depicts Jesus' call to the first four disciples as a summons that elicited the immediate and total abandonment of their way of life. In this encounter between Jesus and the four Galilean fishermen, the call to follow after the Lord results in a spontaneous letting go of a profession, a cherished home, and even blood ties. Jesus' summons produces an almost reckless abandonment of one's established life.

While acknowledging the radical nature of Christ's call to each of his followers, the *Rite of Christian Initiation of Adults* follows an ancient order that honors time as a factor in conversion. The rite is composed of four periods that correspond to the journey of faith development and three steps that ritually make visible and tangible

1. Mark 1:16–20.

All preaching must be oriented with the goal of opening hearts to the mystery and wonder of Christ's call to discipleship.

the movement of the Spirit in the lives of those coming to Christ. The rite states: "This journey includes not only the periods for making inquiry and for maturing, but also the steps marking the catechumens' progress, as they pass, so to speak, through another doorway or ascend to the next level."[2] It is important for pastors and for all those involved in the Christian initiation process to have a solid understanding of these periods and steps in order to allow catechumens to pass through them naturally and at their own pace. Knowledge of the process as a whole will help to prevent rushing men and women to the font without adequate preparation.

Period of Evangelization and Precatechumenate

The Period of Evangelization and Precatechumenate is intended to simply open the hearts of men and women to the call of Christ. During this period, few expectations regarding knowledge of Jesus and the Church are placed on those who have presented themselves as seekers. This time is called "evangelization" because it is precisely about proclaiming the Gospel. The Lord commands the Apostles after his Resurrection: "Go, therefore, and make disciples of all nations, baptizing them in the name of the Father, and of the Son, and of the holy Spirit, and teaching them to observe all that I have commanded you."[3] Pope Paul VI echoes this summons in *Evangelii*

2. RCIA, 6.
3. Matthew 28:19–20.

nuntiandi: "For the Church, evangelizing means bringing the Good News into all the strata of humanity, and through its influence transforming humanity from within and making it new."[4] Most critical during the precatechumenate is to make the voice of Jesus heard and to help inquirers to detect the sound of that voice.

The evangelical nature of this period calls pastors to scrutinize both their commitment to preaching the Gospel in word and in action and the quality of that preaching. It is not necessary for preachers to craft homilies directly for those involved in the precatechumenate; however, the question must always be raised as to how effective preaching is in attracting people to Jesus and in proclaiming the coming of the Kingdom. In other words, all preaching must be oriented to the goal of opening hearts to the mystery and wonder of Christ's call to discipleship. In response to the appearance of inquirers, pastors are regularly challenged to raise the bar of preaching in the parish context.

Furthermore, the *Rite of Christian Initiation of Adults* defines the Period of Evangelization as a time when a person might come to grips with the past sin of his or her life, thereby making the choice to follow Christ one of true freedom. The rite states: "From evangelization, completed with the help of God, come the faith and initial conversion that cause a person to feel called away from sin and drawn into the mystery of God's love."[5] The Period of the Precatechumenate can often be an emotional time for inquirers who wrestle with past demons or who have doubts about their resolve to be truly committed to this new way of life. Due to this emotional turmoil, it is important that pastors generously offer God's mercy to newcomers. This is not to suggest that the Sacrament of Reconciliation is for the unbaptized, but rather, representatives of the Church must be ready to offer their counsel and the mercy of God. Pope Francis has written of the great responsibility to equate evangelization with divine mercy: "The Church is commissioned to announce the mercy of God, the beating heart of the Gospel, which in its own way must penetrate the heart and mind of every person."[6] The Period of Evangelization ought to make very apparent that God's mercy is not a commodity

4. EN, 18.
5. RCIA, 37.
6. MV, 12.

that the Church hoards but is to be extended to every creature under heaven.

Thus, the project of evangelization is not the sole domain of the pastor; it is the responsibility of the Church as a whole. The rite states: "During this period, priests and deacons, catechists and other laypersons are to give the candidates a suitable explanation of the Gospel."[7] While suitable training on how to reflect on God's Word is necessary for the laity working directly with the inquirers, pastors may consider ways to involve the whole parish in evangelization. Perhaps families of the parish who are seen to be role models of Christian fidelity may welcome seekers into their homes for a meal and conversation. Pastors might also consider ways to encourage parishioners to involve those contemplating a relationship with Christ in charitable works. So much of the Gospel can be proclaimed when a witness of Christian charity and love is provided.

The Period of Evangelization and Precatechumenate is not to be governed by a particular time frame. This period is brought to a conclusion with the Rite of Acceptance, which should be celebrated whenever necessary throughout the calendar year. Acceptance should be celebrated when individual inquirers, along with the input of the Christian initiation team, believe themselves to be sufficiently prepared to announce to the Church that they are ready to seek Christ. Therefore, the content of the precatechumenate focuses on general topics such as: the nature of conversion (What does it mean to be called by God? What are the common elements to conversion stories?), the Word of God (What is the nature of the Bible? What images of God are presented in Scripture?), basic experiences of Church (How does Catholicism interpret Christianity? What are various models of the Church?), and prayer (How do Christians pray? What difference does prayer make?). Conversion, Scripture, Church, and prayer—these may be considered the basics to the precatechumenate. These topics may raise deeper questions and/or difficulties in the hearts of inquirers that need resolution before they progress to acceptance.

The RCIA does not prescribe rituals for the Period of Evangelization and Precatechumenate; however, the rite instructs

7. RCIA, 38.

that priests may draw on rituals that are part of the Period of the Catechumenate. "During the precatechumenate period, parish priests (pastors) should help those taking part in it with prayers suited to them, for example, by celebrating for their spiritual well-being the prayers of exorcism and the blessings given in the ritual."[8] While these specific prayers and blessings are to be treated as part of the Period of the Catechumenate, they can certainly be used with seekers during the time of inquiry. The priest who seeks to embody the love and compassion of the Good Shepherd will make himself available for times of prayer within the entire catechumenal process.

Rite of Acceptance into the Order of Catechumens

The Period of Evangelization and Precatechumenate comes to an end with a formal ritual of acceptance into the catechumenate. The timing of the Rite of Acceptance into the Order of Catechumens is based upon the readiness of individual inquirers and involves a change in status for those to be made catechumens, who "should be encouraged to seek blessings and other suffrages from the Church, since they are of the household of Christ; they are entitled to Christian burial should they die before the completion of their initiation."[9] After appropriate discernment with representatives of the Christian initiation team, sponsors, and parish clergy, those who have been exploring the decision to pursue a life in Christ are invited to publicly declare their desire for catechesis. The RCIA states:

> The rite that is called the rite of acceptance into the order of catechumens is of the utmost importance. Assembling publicly for the first time, the candidates who have completed the period of the precatechumenate declare their intention to the Church and the Church in turn, carrying out its apostolic mission, accepts them as persons who intend to become its members. God showers his grace on the candidates, since the celebration manifests their desire publicly and marks their reception and first consecration by the Church.[10]

8. RCIA, 40.
9. NS, 8.
10. RCIA, 41.

Standing before the assembly and declaring the intention to follow Christ can be frightening for those seeking entrance into the catechumenate. Therefore, discerning the readiness of candidates is a particularly important pastoral task for the priests of the parish and other leaders of the Christian initiation process. "Before the rite is celebrated, therefore, sufficient and necessary time, as required in each case, should be set aside to evaluate and, if necessary, to purify the candidates' motives and dispositions."[11] In fact, one of the aspects of discernment that is the responsibility of the priest is to ensure that those entering the catechumenate are truly unbaptized: "[I]t is the duty of parish priests (pastors) to see to it that no baptized person seeks for any reason whatever to be baptized a second time."[12]

When candidates for the catechumenate have discerned their readiness, a time is chosen for the celebration of the Rite of Acceptance. The RCIA offers several suggestions for determining when this is best to be celebrated. The first condition necessary for the celebration of the rite is the display of nascent faith on the part

When readiness has been discerned, a time is chosen for the Rite of Acceptance into the Order of Catechumens.

11. RCIA, 43.

12. RCIA, 43.

of the candidates, who are "to show the first signs of conversion."[13] Secondly, it is recommended that the rite be celebrated with more than one candidate: "In places where the number of candidates is smaller than usual, the rite of acceptance should be delayed until a group is formed that is sufficiently large for catechesis and the liturgical rites."[14] This regulation is theologically valuable, as it serves to remind us that faith development involves a community and can never be a solely private affair. Finally, the RCIA suggests that "two dates in the year, or three if necessary, are to be fixed as the usual times for carrying out this rite."[15] Similar to the recommendation that the Rite of Acceptance be celebrated in groups of two or more candidates, the fixing of dates for the performance of this liturgy helps to underscore that the making of catechumens is done for the good of the entire faith community; the Rite of Acceptance celebrates the action of the candidates giving themselves over to a process beyond their control.

The parish priest is also advised to participate in the preparation of the liturgy during which the Rite of Acceptance will take place. It is the responsibility of the coordinator of the catechumenal process to engage the priest who presides and others who oversee the execution of the liturgy in a complete and thorough preparation of the rite. It is important that the Rite of Acceptance fit in well with the overall schema of the parish's liturgical life. The pastor will have the best understanding of the makeup of the parish to ensure that the "entire Christian community or some part of it, consisting of friends and acquaintances, catechists and priests, take an active part in the celebration."[16]

In preparation for the rite and in presiding over it, the pastor is charged with the responsibility of fully understanding the structure of the liturgy and how it is integrated into the overall celebration of the Eucharist. In choreographing the Rite of Acceptance, the priest will need to carefully consider how to best engage the candidates in a warm and hospitable manner while at the same time taking into consideration the assembly's participation. If the role of

13. RCIA, 18 §1.

14. RCIA, 18 §2.

15. RCIA, 18 §3.

16. RCIA, 45.

the assembly is reduced to the mere observation of a dialogue between the priest and the candidates, the liturgy will not be as effective as intended. To best integrate the flow of the rite into the Eucharistic liturgy as a whole, it is helpful to consider its primary symbols as well as the gestures and movements envisioned by the rite.

The structure of the Rite of Acceptance into the Order of Catechumens is as follows:

Receiving the Candidates

- Greeting
- Opening Dialogue
- Candidates First Acceptance of the Gospel
- Affirmation by the Sponsors and the Assembly
- Signing of the Candidates with the Cross
    - Signing of the Forehead
    - Signing of the Other Senses (optional)
    - Concluding Prayer
- Invitation to the Celebration of the Word of God

Liturgy of the Word

- Instruction
- Readings
- Homily
- Presentation of a Bible (optional)
- Intercessions for the Catechumens
- Prayer over the Catechumens
- Dismissal of the Catechumens

Liturgy of the Eucharist

The Rite of Acceptance into the Order of Catechumens ideally begins outside the church. Given that this is a threshold ritual meant to demonstrate the movement of seekers into a new world, the physical door of the church building is an important symbol of transition. The pastor may wish to invite members of the assembly to gather with candidates in the portico or gathering space of the church, where the "assembly of the faithful may sing a psalm or an appropriate song."[17]

17. RCIA, 48.

What is most crucial is that those gathered outside and those remaining inside the church be able to see and to hear the liturgical action.

This action begins with the presider greeting the candidates. The tone of this greeting is not to be taken lightly. It matters a great deal that the pastor extend warmth, hospitality, and eagerness to receive new life into the Church. The RCIA states:

> The celebrant greets the candidates in a friendly manner. He speaks to them, their sponsors, and all present, pointing out the joy and happiness of the Church. He may also recall for the sponsors and friends the particular experience and religious response by which the candidates, following their own spiritual path, have come to this first step.[18]

The presider may wish to point out to the community that the men and women who have come to be accepted by the Church have invested time and energy, discernment and prayer into the decision to stand before the assembly. The pastor may also desire to provide words that validate the action of God in the hearts of the candidates. The Rite of Acceptance is not intended to be a reward for personal merit but instead is to manifest the power of God's Word to entice hearers to respond.

After the initial greeting, the presider asks the candidates their names and inquires as to why they have come. Even if there are many candidates, each should be allowed to state his or her name publicly and to respond individually to the question "What do you ask of God's Church?" The rite suggests that the presider may tailor this question in another suitable way: "The celebrant may use other words than those provided in asking the candidates about their intentions and may let them answer in their own words."[19] For example, the presider may ask quite simply "Why have you come here?" If the candidates have not been instructed to formally respond with the answer "faith," then the presider should be prepared to respond to the answers in an appropriate way, attempting to steer the response in the direction of "eternal life" or "life in Christ" or another answer that suggests the desire for faith.

Given that the Church is called to witness in this public ritual the sowing of the seeds of faith in the hearts of those seeking

18. RCIA, 49.

19. RCIA, 50.

to enter the order of catechumens, it is a striking gesture that they are now asked to accept the Gospel for the first time. Continuing to stand within the doorway of the church, the presider addresses the candidates, adapting one of three formularies.[20] Option C offers a challenge to those who accept the way of the Gospel:

> This is eternal life: to know the one true God and Jesus Christ, whom he has sent. Christ has been raised from the dead and appointed by God as the Lord of life and ruler of all things, seen and unseen.
>
> If, then, you wish to become his disciples and members of his Church, you must be guided to the fullness of the truth that he has revealed to us. You must learn to make the mind of Christ Jesus your own. You must strive to pattern your life on the teachings of the Gospel and so to love the Lord your God and your neighbor. For this was Christ's command and he was its perfect example.
>
> Is each of you ready to accept these teachings of the Gospel?

To this brief explanation of the demands of embracing the Good News, the candidates reply "I am." Then the presider turns to the sponsors and to the entire assembly and asks: "Sponsors, you now present these candidates to us; are you, and all who are gathered here with us, ready to help these candidates find and follow Christ?"[21] Once again, a positive affirmation is expected.

The need for the affirmation of the sponsors in this rite has foundations in the early Church, when sponsors assumed the crucial role of testifying that those seeking to enter the community were trustworthy and were not there to do harm to the Christian Church. This approval of those to be made catechumens is echoed by the presider's words of praise:

> Father of mercy,
> we thank you for these your servants.
> You have sought and summoned them in many ways
> and they have turned to seek you.
>
> You have called them today
> and they have answered in our presence:
> we praise you, Lord, and we bless you.[22]

---

20. RCIA, 52.
21. RCIA, 53.
22. RCIA, 53.

The Church has much to be thankful for as it witnesses the initial desire for faith on the part of the inquirers. Such desire calls the faithful to recognize God's activity in their lives as well, for God has "sought and summoned" all those who hear his voice. The assembly, therefore, stamps the final words of the presider, saying or singing: "We praise you, Lord, and we bless you."

The next ritual element of the Rite of Acceptance into the Order of Catechumens is the signing of the candidates with the cross. While this is intended to be performed in the gathering space of the Church, it may be preferable to move the candidates into the body of the church, allowing for the visual participation of the entire assembly. If there is one main aisle in the church, presiders may wish to have the candidates stagger themselves throughout the aisle. The following instructions are provided for the tracing of the cross: "Next the cross is traced on the forehead of the candidates . . . at the discretion of the celebrant the signing of one, several, or all of the senses may follow. The celebrant alone says the formularies accompanying each signing."[23] For the signing of the forehead, two formularies are provided and are to be used according to the number of candidates involved. With option A, the presider, as well as the

The signing of the senses calls attention to the sacredness of the person.

23. RCIA, 54.

sponsors, marks each candidate with the Sign of the Cross, and the presider says, "N., receive the cross on your forehead. It is Christ himself who now strengthens you with this sign of his love. Learn to know him and follow him."[24] The assembly responds with a sung acclamation or a proclamation of praise such as "Glory and praise to you, Lord Jesus Christ!" In option B, the presider makes the Sign of the Cross over the candidates as a group, while the sponsors or catechists trace the cross on the forehead of each candidate.

The signing of the other senses appears as an optional component in the Rite of Acceptance. However, its importance is not to be missed. First of all, it invites greater participation in the ritual for the sponsors and catechists, as they are intended to be the ones to mark the individual senses of the candidates.[25] More importantly, signing all of the senses calls attention to the sacredness of the person as a whole and the fact that the entire body is engaged in the process of conversion. It is not only the mind and the heart that come to Christ, but the feet and the hands as well. The rich imagery that accompanies the signing is clearly seen below:

> While the ears are being signed, the celebrant says:
> Receive the sign of the cross on your ears,
> that you may hear the voice of the Lord.
>
> While the eyes are being signed:
> Receive the sign of the cross on your eyes,
> that you may see the glory of God.
>
> While the lips are being signed:
> Receive the sign of the cross on your lips,
> that you may respond to the word of God.
>
> While the breast is being signed:
> Receive the sign of the cross over your heart,
> that Christ may dwell there by faith.
>
> While the shoulders are being signed:
> Receive the sign of the cross on your shoulders,
> that you may bear the gentle yoke of Christ.

24. RCIA, 55.
25. RCIA, 56.

[While the hands are being signed:

Receive the sign of the cross on your hands,
that Christ may be known in the work which you do.

While the feet are being signed:
Receive the sign of the cross on your feet,
that you may walk in the way of Christ.][26]

The rite brackets the final two signings, the signing of the hands and the signing of the feet, showing that they are optional. Because the hands and the feet are so commonly understood as body parts to be used in the way of Christian discipleship, it seems most appropriate that, at the very least, these should be marked with the Sign of the Cross. The presider now makes a final Sign of the Cross over the group or before each candidate (if they are few in numbers) and says: "I sign you with the sign of eternal life in the name of the Father, and of the Son, and of the Holy Spirit." The newly made catechumens respond "Amen." The signing of the forehead (and the senses) ends with a concluding prayer. Two options are provided; option A reads as follows:

Lord,
we have signed these catechumens
with the sign of Christ's cross.

Protect them by its power,
so that, faithful to the grace which has begun in them,
they may keep your commandments
and come to the glory of rebirth in baptism.
We ask this through Christ our Lord.[27]

Optional rites are provided that also may take place before the presider invites the catechumens to listen to the Word of God. It makes sense for the "Presentation of a Cross"[28] to occur at the conclusion of the signing, but it may take place at the conclusion of the Liturgy of the Word. While the cross is presented, the priest states: "You have been marked with the cross of Christ. Receive now the sign of his love." The other optional rite, the "Giving of a New

26. RCIA, 56.

27. RCIA, 57.

28. RCIA, 74.

Name," is rarely executed in the United States and is done only with the approval of the local bishop. A new name may be given to catechumens "from cultures in which it is the practice of non-Christian religions to give a new name."[29]

After the signing and optional rites, the ritual text envisions the catechumens entering the body of the church for the first time: "The celebrant next invites the catechumens and their sponsors to enter the church (or the place where the liturgy of the word will be celebrated)."[30] Calling the catechumens by name, the presider invites them to participate in the hearing of God's Word: "N. and N., come into the church, to share with us at the table of God's word."[31] The tenderness by which the priest is to treat these men and women, who are new to listening to the Word of God, is inferred in paragraph 61: "After the catechumens have reached their places, the celebrant speaks to them briefly, helping them to understand the dignity of God's word, which is proclaimed and heard in the church."[32] This same paragraph also indicates that the presider may wish to honor the Word of God by incensing the *Book of the Gospels* that is used in the celebration of the Word. The readings are then proclaimed and explained by the homily that follows. After the homily, an optional rite is provided whereby a Bible or a book containing the Gospels may be presented to the candidates.[33] If used, the presider presents the book to each catechumen, saying, "Receive the Gospel of Jesus Christ, the Son of God."

The Liturgy of the Word comes to a conclusion with intercessions for the catechumens. If the catechumens are to be dismissed from the assembly immediately afterward, the intercessions are to be supplemented with "intentions for the Church and the whole world."[34] The priest's invitation to the intercessions acknowledges the persevering spirit of the catechumens who have journeyed to this point: "These catechumens, who are our brothers and sisters, have already traveled a long road. We rejoice with them in the gentle

29. RCIA, 73.
30. RCIA, 60.
31. RCIA, 60.
32. RCIA, 61.
33. RCIA, 64.
34. RCIA, 65.

guidance of God who has brought them to this day. Let us pray that they may press onwards, until they come to share fully in our way of life." The intercessions conclude with one of two choices for a prayer over the catechumens. For example, the priest, with hands outstretched over the catechumens, may pray:

> Almighty God,
> source of all creation,
> you have made us in your image.
> Welcome with love those who come before you today.
>
> They have listened among us to the word of Christ;
> by its power renew them
> and by your grace refashion them,
> so that in time they may assume the full likeness of Christ,
> who lives and reigns for ever and ever.[35]

The Body of Christ has changed in the course of the Rite of Acceptance into the Order of Catechumens. Those who have been accepted as catechumens are now to be called members of the household of Christ, and they have the right to be married in the Church and to be buried from the Church. Their listening for the first time to the "word of Christ" within the assembly of the faithful represents an important point of passage on their journey of conversion.

This rite is also the first time they will be dismissed from the Eucharistic assembly. The dismissal has long been understood not as a form of punishment to deprive the unbaptized from the Table of the Lord but rather as the means of protecting them from mysteries surpassing their ability to comprehend. The rite provides the following instruction on their dismissal:

> The celebrant recalls briefly the great joy with which the catechumens have just been received and urges them to live according to the word of God they have just heard. After the dismissal formulary, the group of catechumens goes out but does not disperse. With the help of some of the faithful, the catechumens remain together to share their joy and spiritual experiences.[36]

35. RCIA, 66.
36. RCIA, 67.

Notice that the presider is encouraged to articulate the "great joy" that has just been experienced by the Church. Such articulation will help to impress upon the newly made catechumens that they are indeed providing a noble ministry for the Church by entering into an "order" that witnesses to conversion. The dismissal may be taken from the two formularies provided or may be crafted in similar words. These formularies are: "Catechumens, go in peace, and may the Lord remains with you always" and "My dear friends, this community now sends you forth to reflect more deeply upon the word of God which you have shared with us today. Be assured of our loving support and prayers for you. We look forward to the day when you will share fully in the Lord's Table." Although considerably longer, the second option seems preferable, as it emphasizes the ongoing relationship between the assembly and the catechumens. If the Liturgy of the Eucharist follows, the general intercessions should be prayed for the Church and the whole world. However, both these intercessions and the Profession of Faith may be omitted for pastoral reasons.[37] The Liturgy of the Eucharist proceeds as usual.

A final note must be inserted here regarding the optional rites that fall at the end of this "first step." Previously mentioned were the two optional rites: the Giving of a New Name and the Presentation of a Cross. However, the RCIA also makes use here of a possible "Exorcism and Renunciation of False Worship." The inclusion of first exorcism and renunciation of false worship is at the discretion of the diocesan bishop.[38] Pastors ought to be able to detect the difference between this exorcism and those that take place within the catechumenate and the scrutinies during the Period of Purification and Enlightenment. Two rubrics within this rite make certain the uniqueness of the "false worship" that is to be countered:

> In regions where false worship is widespread, whether in worshiping spiritual powers or in calling on the shades of the dead or in using magical arts, the diocesan bishop may permit the introduction of a first exorcism and a renunciation of false worship; this replaces the candidates' first acceptance of the Gospel.[39]

37. RCIA, 68.
38. RCIA, 33 §2.
39. RCIA, 70.

and

> After giving a brief introduction to the rite, the celebrant breathes lightly toward the face of each candidate and, with a symbolic gesture, for example, holding up his right hand, or without any gesture, says the formulary of exorcism.[40]

Some sort of practice in the art of witchcraft or sorcery is the type of evil that is intended to be rooted out of the candidates with this rite. The words of the presider suggest the true presence of evil, almost demonic possession:

> By the breath of your mouth, O Lord,
> drive away the spirits of evil.
> Command them to depart,
> for your kingdom has come among us.[41]

The exorcism is followed up by a renunciation of false worship. It is the role of the diocesan bishop to ensure the preparation of a formulary for the questions that are asked of candidates so as to maintain their relevance to the local situation.[42] The RCIA provides two such formularies that ask candidates to reject "those powers that are not of God and those forms of worship that do not rightly honor him." It is important to underscore the fact that it is necessary for pastors to receive the permission of the diocesan bishop before this rite is celebrated within the context of the Rite of Acceptance into the Order of Catechumens. This is clearly meant to be an "extra"-ordinary ritual, mostly to be used in lands that are largely unaware of the Gospel.

40. RCIA, 71.

41. RCIA, 71.

42. RCIA, 72.

Chapter Four

Second Period / Second Step: Catechumenate and Election

After a time of seeking, men and women who have entered the Order of Catechumens can be understood as apprentices. Unlike students, who might see their task as that of acquiring information, apprentices exhibit a commitment to train to have skills engrained within their bodies. Christian disciples apprentice to grow into Christ and his Body, the Church. Perhaps the earliest Christians in Jerusalem after Jesus' Death and Resurrection understood themselves as apprentices with certain skills to master. As is recorded in the Acts of the Apostles:

> The community of believers was of one heart and mind, and no one claimed that any of his possessions was his own, but they had everything in common. With great power the apostles bore witness to the resurrection of the Lord Jesus, and great favor was accorded them all. There was no needy person among them, for those who owned property or houses would sell them, bring the proceeds of the sale, and put them at the feet of the apostles, and they were distributed to each according to need.[1]

1. Acts 4:32–35.

Certainly this behavior did not just come naturally to these citizens of Jerusalem; it had to be put on and practiced. While this ideal portrayal of the Church undoubtedly masks its flaws, it clearly suggests that the Apostles' preaching kept the memory of the Lord alive, and in turn, inspired the community to live as one. This is really what the Period of the Catechumenate is all about: coming to faith in Christ by hearing the Word and participating in the life of the community.

Thus, paragraph 75 of the RCIA rightly defines the catechumenate as "an extended period during which the candidates are given suitable pastoral formation and guidance, aimed at training them in the Christian life."[2] Notice this description does not use the words *education* or *instruction*, but rather *formation, guidance,* and *training.* While the precatechumenate is designed to introduce inquirers into the basics of believing in God, general habits of discernment, and the attitudes of prayer, the catechumenate immerses candidates into the specifics of the Catholic faith without taking on the atmosphere of a classroom. By the time this period of formation ends, and each of the catechumens will have been observed in terms of their apprenticeship, making them truly credible in taking a further step on their way to Baptism, namely that of election, or of being chosen for Christ.

Period of the Catechumenate

Paragraph 75 continues to reveal that Christian formation is to unfold according to four means. First, the catechumenate is to provide a "suitable catechesis," that is "gradual and complete in its coverage" and that is "accommodated to the liturgical year."[3] It is important to note that the catechesis envisioned in the ritual text does not revolve simply upon the transmission of dogmas and precepts but hopes to plunge candidates into contemplation of the mystery of salvation as a whole. Second, the catechumenate seeks to help catechumens develop prayer lives that are thoroughly Christian and are intrinsically related to their love of neighbor. Third, the catechumenate provides for moments of celebrating liturgical rites

2. RCIA, 75.

3. RCIA, 75 §1.

"which purify the catechumens little by little and strengthen them with God's blessing."[4] Finally, the Period of the Catechumenate opens the eyes and hearts of catechumens to the apostolic mission of the Church as they "learn how to work actively with others to spread the Gospel and build up the Church by the witness of their lives and by professing their faith." In sum, the four ways of educating the mind and the heart during the Period of the Catechumenate center on catechesis, prayer, liturgical rites, and apostolic ministry.

Given the nature of these four areas for growth and maturity on the part of catechumens within the broader goal of developing Christian disciples, it might be appropriate to scrutinize the setting for the catechumenate. Too often the sessions for catechesis take on the feel of a classroom, and catechumens come believing that they are to receive information. However, this is not the spirit of the Rite of Christian Initiation of Adults. As stated previously, the training catechumens are to receive is to be an apprenticeship; it is hands-on learning that involves the investment of the heart as well as the head. Therefore, while a formal outline for the dogmatic material to be covered during the course of the catechumenate is necessary, it is important to keep this in check with the movement of the Spirit, or in the words of the RCIA: "Nothing, therefore, can be settled *a priori*."[5] Catechumenal gatherings ought to take place in a wide variety of settings beyond the traditional classroom, from the church building to public settings such as parks or workplaces to the homes of the catechumens themselves. By attempting to broaden the stage upon which faith is shared, catechumens will be led to understand faith as a communal endeavor that touches upon every aspect of life.

As with the precatechumenate, the Period of the Catechumenate is meant to last as long as is necessary for real conversion to take place. It is often the case that, in keeping with the secular calendar, the catechumenate begins in the fall of the year and continues to the beginning of Lent. Is this designation of a mere three to four months sufficient for a true change of heart? The RCIA offers this instruction:

---

4. RCIA, 75 §3.
5. RCIA, 76.

> The time spent in the catechumenate should be long enough—several years if necessary—for the conversion and faith of the catechumens to become strong. By their formation in the entire Christian life and a sufficiently prolonged probation the catechumens are properly initiated into the mysteries of salvation and the practice of an evangelical way of life.[6]

While it is ultimately the bishop who determines the duration and the content of the catechumenate,[7] the pastor works with the catechumenal team to support both the discernment of the catechumens as they consider their readiness to continue to the Easter sacraments and provides input on the contents of the faith being disseminated through catechesis. Given his leadership role in the parish and his representation of the local bishop, the pastor has the duty to guarantee that catechesis is holistic, grounded in tradition, and theologically sound. The RCIA states: "The instruction that the catechumens receive during this period should be of a kind that while presenting Catholic teaching in its entirely also enlightens faith, directs the heart toward God, fosters participation in the liturgy, inspires apostolic activity, and nurtures a life completely in accord with the spirit of Christ."[8]

During the Period of the Catechumenate, the pastor has the opportunity to participate with the catechumens in a host of liturgical rites, such as celebrations of the Word of God, blessings, minor exorcisms, and anointings.[9] Among these rites, celebrations of the Word of God are to be considered "foremost."[10] These celebrations are: (1) prepared specially for the catechumens, (2) participation in the Liturgy of the Word in the Sunday assembly, and (3) celebrations connected to catechetical instruction. While celebrations of the Word of God often take place without the involvement of the pastor, such opportunities to share God's Word and to provide a homily are in keeping with priestly ministry. Since the model for a celebration of the Word of God[11] (RCIA, 85–89) suggests that its conclusion may include a minor exorcism or a blessing of the catechumens, it is good

6. RCIA, 76.

7. RCIA, 77.

8. RCIA, 78.

9. RCIA, 79.

10. RCIA, 79.

11. RCIA, 85–89.

for the pastor to take part in celebrations of the Word of God as frequently as possible.

Minor exorcisms may also be employed during the Period of the Catechumenate. "They draw the attention of the catechumens to the real nature of Christian life, the struggle between flesh and spirit, the importance of self-denial for reaching the blessedness of God's kingdom, and the unending need for God's help."[12] The word *exorcism* tends to be equated with the Devil and demonic possession and often goes unused. However, minor exorcisms can be grace-filled moments of encounter with the divine. They are simple in their format, as they entail only the utterance of a prayer over the catechumens, who either bow or kneel before the presider. One of the eleven prayers of exorcism that the RCIA offers reads as follows:

> Lord Jesus Christ,
> when you climbed the mountain to preach,
> you turned your disciples from the paths of sin
> and revealed to them the beatitudes of your kingdom.

The pastor has the duty to guarantee that catechesis is holistic, grounded in tradition, and theologically sound.

12. RCIA, 90.

Help these your servants, who hear the word of the Gospel,
and protect them from the spirit of greed, of lust, and of pride.
May they find the blessings of your kingdom
in poverty and in hunger,
in mercy and in purity of heart.
May they work for peace and joyfully endure persecution
and so come to share your kingdom
and experience the mercy you promised.
May they finally see God in the joy of heaven
where you live and reign for ever and ever. Amen.[13]

This prayer reads as a standard blessing prayer that could conclude any liturgical event. There is nothing in the minor exorcisms that should prevent their use. In fact, they should be employed often throughout the catechumenate. "A minor exorcism may also be held at the beginning or end of a meeting for catechesis."[14] Thus, a busy pastor could be present at either end of a session and offer to lead the group in a prayer seeking God's mercy.

Through blessings, the Church offers the catechumens courage, joy, and peace during their journey.

Since the RCIA also offers the opportunities for blessings, how do these differ from the minor exorcisms? While the minor exorcisms are intended to alert catechumens to the struggle involved in the Christian way of life, blessings "are bestowed on the catechumens so that, even though they do not as yet have the grace of the sacraments, they may still receive from the Church courage, joy, and peace as they proceed along the difficult journey they have begun."[15] The Book of Blessings, which governs the official actions of blessing people,

13. RCIA, 94, RCIA, 89, Option D.

14. RCIA, 92.

15. RCIA, 96.

objects, and events, states: "Whether God blessed the people himself or through the ministry of those who acted in his name, his blessing was always a promise of divine help, a proclamation of his favor, a reassurance of his faithfulness."[16] Thus, blessings during the catechumenate differ from minor exorcisms primarily by their positive nature of God's love rather than human sinfulness.

Just as catechumens are seen to be growing in faith, the praying of blessings is a sign of faith in a God who provides with abundance. The RCIA provides nine blessing prayers to be used during a ritual blessing. Unlike the minor exorcisms, the rite does not suggest that the catechumens bow their heads or kneel before the presider, and the blessings include a silent laying on of hands by the celebrant. The presider at the blessings may be a priest, a deacon, or a qualified and trained catechist who has been appointed by the bishop.[17]

Another liturgical rite belonging to the Period of the Catechumenate, in which the pastor is invited to take part, is the anointing of catechumens. Anointing with the oil of catechumens is a way of visibly marking those undergoing conversion. "The anointing with oil symbolizes their [catechumens] need for God's help and strength so that, undeterred by the bonds of the past and overcoming the opposition of the devil, they will forthrightly take the step of professing their faith and will hold fast to it unfalteringly throughout their lives."[18] Just as oil is understood in common use as a means of protection and strength, so too is the oil of catechumens to bestow a sign of God's favor and care.

The RCIA instructs that the anointing of catechumens take place within the context of a celebration of the Word of God after the homily.[19] While pastoral reasons may permit priests or deacons to anoint individuals privately, a communal celebration of anointing is considered normative and may be celebrated "several times" during the catechumenate.[20] Again, for pastoral reasons, a priest may decide to bless the oil during the anointing rather than to use the oil blessed

---

16. *Book of Blessings*, 6.

17. RCIA, 96.

18. RCIA, 99.

19. RCIA, 100.

20. RCIA, 100.

by the bishop at the Chrism Mass, in which case the words of the blessing provide rich insight into the powerful impact of anointing:

> O God,
> source of strength and defender of your people,
> you have chosen to make this oil,
> created by your hand,
> an effective sign of your power.
>
> Bless + this oil
> and strengthen the catechumens who will be anointed with it.
> Grant them your wisdom to understand the Gospel more deeply
> and your strength to accept the challenges of Christian life.
>
> Enable them to rejoice in baptism
> and to partake of a new life in the Church
> as true children of your family.
>
> We ask this through Christ our Lord.[21]

The anointing marks those undergoing conversion.

After naming God as the "source of strength and defender" of those who believe in him, the prayer continues to develop a theme of strength, adding the gift of "wisdom" for the sake of the Gospel. This rite clearly envisions celebrating a deeper sense of belonging in the family of the Church for those anointed with the oil of catechumens.

Thus, the anointing of catechumens opens with the priest or deacon praying the prayer of exorcism over the candidates. This prayer alludes to Jesus' entering the synagogue in his hometown

21. RCIA, 102.

and proclaiming the prophecy of Isaiah: "The Spirit of the Lord is upon me, because he has anointed me to bring glad tidings to the poor" (Luke 4:18). The prayer asks that God may help the catechumens "grasp" his "moments of grace" and that they may "submit themselves to the power of grace" in the spirit of liberating captives and announcing a "season of forgiveness."[22] Although the ritual provides only one prayer of exorcism, the rubrics suggest that any of the eleven prayers provided in paragraph 94 may be used.[23] If the priest makes the decision to bless the oil during the anointing, rather than to use the oil of the catechumens blessed by the bishop, then the prayer of blessing over the oil takes the place of the prayer of exorcism.

The anointing proceeds with the words that accompany the anointing of children at infant Baptism: "We anoint you with the oil of salvation in the name of Christ our Savior. May he strengthen you with his power, who lives and reigns for ever and ever."[24] The presider then anoints each catechumen individually with the oil on the breast or on both hands, or even on other parts of the body. In determining the appropriate place on the body to anoint, the question might be asked: What part of the body is most in need of God's strength? Because the symbol behind anointing on the breastbone developed around the imagery of a shield put on to do battle, the body part chosen ought to be linked to what is most in need of God's protection. This is not to equate the anointing of catechumens with the anointing of the sick; however, the aim is to draw recipients deeper into the working of God's mercy in their lives.

One of the nine blessings from paragraph 97 may conclude the anointing. The role of the pastor in leading the community in a prayer of exorcism, in physically anointing each catechumen, and in uttering a blessing on their behalf is powerful indeed. To perform this liturgical task well, the priest or deacon ought to be aware of how the gesture of anointing is performed. If an abundance of oil is employed for the anointing, one may argue that the imaginations of the catechumens may be sparked to feel on their bodies God's strengthening and his power. If this gesture is hurried or performed

22. RCIA, 102.

23. RCIA, 102.

24. RCIA, 103.

in a manner of great efficiency, the symbolic weight of the anointing may be lost.

The Presentations of the Creed and the Lord's Prayer are two of the liturgical celebrations considered optional during the catechumenate.[25] The normal placement of the presentations in the schema of the *Rite of Christian Initiation of Adults* is during the season of Lent; however, pastoral reasons may dictate transferring the presentations to the Period of the Catechumenate. The rite states:

> The presentations normally take place during Lent, the period of purification and enlightenment, after the first and third scrutinies. But for pastoral advantage and because the period of purification and enlightenment is rather short, the presentations may be held during the period of the catechumenate, rather than at the regular times. But the presentations are not to take place until a point during the catechumenate when the catechumens are judged ready for these celebrations.[26]

It is not merely the short time span of Lent that may serve as a pastoral reason for transferring the presentations to the Period of the Catechumenate, rather, these celebrations may be used as a "rite of passage."[27] In other words, if catechumens have demonstrated a level of faith development that suggests a true relationship with Christ and a deepened commitment to the Church, the handing over of the Creed and the Lord's Prayer during the catechumenate itself may be very appropriate. The presentations will be treated in greater detail in the next chapter.

Another liturgical celebration that is provided in the RCIA, but is considered an optional rite for use in the Church in the United States, is the Sending of the Catechumens for Election. Because the Rite of Election entails catechumens from around the diocese being received into the elect by the bishop, it is generally difficult for the parish as a whole to participate actively in this celebration. Thus, the Rite of Sending provides the local community with the opportunity to officially affirm the choice that both the catechumens and the Church are making. The rite specifies:

---

25. RCIA, 105.
26. RCIA, 104.
27. RCIA, 21.

> As the focal point of the Church's concern for the catechumens, admission to election belongs to the bishop who is usually its presiding celebrant. It is within the parish community, however, that the preliminary judgment is made concerning the catechumens' state of formation and progress.
>
> This rite offers that local community the opportunity to express its approval of the catechumens and to send them forth to the celebration of election assured of the parish's care and support.[28]

While the bishop is indeed the chief pastor of the diocese, there is something very important about the local parish celebrating the election of its catechumens under the leadership of the pastor. Celebrating the Rite of Sending of the Catechumens for Election can be a powerful experience of the unity of the parish in the context of the universality of the Church.

The Rite of Sending usually takes place on the First Sunday of Lent, immediately prior to the Rite of Election with the bishop. This optional rite begins with the presentation of the catechumens after the homily.[29] It is the role of the pastor to receive for election the catechumens, who are presented by "the priest in charge of the catechumens' initiation, or a deacon, or a catechist, or a representative of the community."[30] After this general presentation, the presider calls the catechumens forward, one by one: "Those who are to be sent to the celebration of election in Christ, come forward, together with those who will be your godparents."[31] Each of the catechumens is called by name, and, accompanied by their godparents, they proceed forward to stand before the presider. Since some catechumens may continue to feel on the fringe of the community at this stage in their formation, it is important for the presider to embody a warm sense of welcome as the catechumens gather before him. For this reason, presiders may wish to stand in the midst of the assembly and invite the catechumens to face the community as a whole, thereby increasing the sense of connectedness between the catechumens and the parish family.

---

28. RCIA, 107.
29. RCIA, 111.
30. RCIA, 111.
31. RCIA, 111.

The signing of one's name in the Book of the Elect heralds the response to Christ's invitation to be baptized in his name.

After their presentation, the pastor calls for the affirmation of the godparents and the entire assembly as to the spiritual preparedness of the catechumens. The presider addresses the gathered church in these or similar words: "My dear friends, these catechumens who have been preparing for the sacraments of initiation hope that they will be found ready to participate in the rite of election and be chosen in Christ for the Easter sacraments. It is the responsibility of this community to inquire about their readiness before they are presented to the bishop."[32] He then addresses the godparents directly and asks them to testify that the catechumens have been sufficiently formed in the Gospel and in the Catholic way of life, that they display conversion in their lives, and that they are ready for election by the bishop.

It is then desirable for the catechumens to sign the Book of the Elect in the presence of the assembly, unless it is to be signed before the bishop.[33] The signing of one's name in this book, filled with the names of men and women from past years, is a powerful gesture of humility. When the signing takes place within the context of the Rite of Election, in the presence of the bishop, catechumens hear a clear summons: "Since you have already heard the call of Christ, you

32. RCIA, 112.

33. RCIA, 113.

must now express your response to that call clearly and in the presence of the whole Church."[34] The Rite of Sending does not provide words to accompany the signing of names, and so the act of giving one's name over in a signature is intended to herald the response to Christ's invitation to be baptized into his name.

The presider then leads the community in intercessions for the catechumens. He invites the assembly to pray in these or similar words:

> My brothers and sisters, we look forward to celebrating at Easter the life-giving mysteries of our Lord's suffering, death and resurrection. As we journey together to the Easter sacraments, these catechumens will look to us for an example of Christian renewal. Let us pray to the Lord for them and for ourselves, that we may be renewed by one another's efforts and together come to share the joys of Easter.

At the conclusion of the intercessions, which ask that the catechumens "may be freed from selfishness and learn to put others first," that their godparents "may be living examples of the Gospel," that their catechists "may always convey to them the beauty of God's word," and that the community "may grow in charity and be constant in prayer," the presider prays a final prayer with hands outstretched over the catechumens, who stand before him:

> Father of love and power,
> it is your will to establish everything in Christ
> and to draw us into his all-embracing love.
>
> Guide these catechumens in the days and weeks ahead:
> strengthen them in their vocation,
> build them into the kingdom of your Son,
> and seal them with the Spirit of your promise.
>
> We ask this through Christ our Lord.[35]

At the conclusion of this prayer, the presider dismisses the catechumens from the assembly, as has been the custom throughout the Period of the Catechumenate, and the Mass proceeds with the Liturgy of the Eucharist. As they have done together for many months, the catechumens are dismissed from the assembly to reflect upon

34. RCIA, 132.

35. RCIA, 115.

the Word of God. After the sending rite, they will certainly have much to reflect on regarding the seriousness of their commitment to baptized life as well as the affirmation of the parish community. The dismissal takes this or a similar form:

> My dear friends, you are about to set out on the road that leads to the glory of Easter. Christ will be your way, your truth, and your life. In his name we send you forth from this community to celebrate with the bishop the Lord's choice of you to be numbered among his elect. Until we meet again for the scrutinies, walk always in his peace.36

Rite of Election or Enrollment of Names

The Rite of Election serves as a key rite of passage in the process of conversion. Having spent many hours in formal instruction, prayer, and discernment—"the lengthy period of formation of the catechumens' minds and hearts"—catechumens make the transition from the Order of Catechumens to that of the Elect.[37] Once again, these men and women provide a ministry to the Church as a whole, as they witness to God's mercy and to the strength of Christ's call to discipleship. Usually taking place on the First Sunday of Lent, this ritual marks the beginning of the final period of the Christian initiation process, that of Purification and Enlightenment:

> At this second step, on the basis of the testimony of godparents and catechists and of the catechumens' reaffirmation of their intention, the Church judges their state of readiness and decides on their advancement toward the sacraments of initiation. Thus the Church makes its "election," that is the choice and admission of those catechumens who have the dispositions that make them fit to take part, at the next major celebration, in the sacraments of initiation.
>
> This step is called election because the acceptance made by the Church is founded on the election by God, in whose name the Church acts. The step is also called the enrollment of names because as a pledge of fidelity the candidates inscribe their names in the book that lists those who have been chosen for initiation.[38]

36. RCIA, 116.
37. RCIA, 118.
38. RCIA, 119.

Reaching this stage in their journey, those participating in election will experience a change in their status in the Church: "From the day of their election and admission, the catechumens are called 'the elect.' They are also described as *competentes* ('co-petitioners'), because they are joined together in asking for and aspiring to receive the three sacraments of Christ and the gift of the Holy Spirit."[39] This same paragraph continues to describe the change that takes place as men and women cross from being catechumens to being chosen by the Church: "They are also called *illuminandi* ('those who will be enlightened'), because baptism itself has been called *illuminatio* ('enlightenment') and it fills the newly baptized with the light of faith."[40]

While the Rite of Election or Enrollment of Names largely focuses on the catechumens and the presiding bishop, the work of the catechumenal team and the parish as a whole serves as the necessary framework for this ritual celebration. In other words, the Body of Christ has facilitated the formation of men and women who are chosen to be one with the Body, and it will continue to guide and nurture them as they are drawn more deeply into Christ who stirs up life-giving waters. The rite states:

> Before the rite of election the bishop, priests, deacons, catechists, godparents, and the entire community, in accord with their respective responsibilities and in their own way, should, after considering the matter carefully, arrive at a judgment about the catechumens' state of formation and progress. After the election, they should surround the elect with prayer, so that the entire Church will accompany and lead them to encounter Christ.[41]

Therefore, it is the duty of the pastor to encourage the parish to participate in the Rite of Election. At the very least, the parish designates representatives to attend the celebration and to return to the parish with an account of what they witnessed. The pastor must consider carefully the way in which this ritual is not simply isolated to the confines of the cathedral but rather plays a continuing role in the ongoing call of evangelization to the whole parish to embrace transformation into Christ as a baptismal, and therefore daily, responsibility.

---

39. RCIA, 124.
40. RCIA, 124.
41. RCIA, 121.

The structure for the Rite of Election is as follows:

Liturgy of the Word

- Homily
- Presentation of the Catechumens
- Affirmation by the Godparents [and the Assembly]
- Invitation and Enrollment of Names
- Act of Admission or Election
- Intercessions for the Elect
- Prayer over the Elect
- Dismissal of the Elect

Liturgy of the Eucharist

The RCIA instructs that the Rite of Election normally take place during Mass;[42] however, given that many parishes celebrate the Rite of Sending immediately prior to the gathering with the bishop, many dioceses celebrate it outside the context of Mass within a celebration of the Word of God. Within or outside Mass, the Rite of Election or Enrollment of Names takes place after the bishop's homily. According to the ritual, it may be the pastor or "the priest in charge of the catechumens' initiation, or a deacon, a catechist, or a representative of the community" who presents the catechumens to the bishop.[43] As in the Rite of Sending, the catechumens are to be called by name and are to assemble before the bishop, who, in the act of affirmation, has been made aware of the catechumens' suitability to be declared as "elect" and thus presents the catechumens to the assembly (option A) or seeks to determine the preparedness of the catechumens by questioning their godparents (option B). In the case of the former, the bishop addresses the assembly and the godparents in these or similar words:

> My dear friends, these catechumens have asked to be initiated into the sacramental life of the Church this Easter. Those who know them have judged them to be sincere in their desire. During the period of their preparation they have listened to the word of Christ and endeavored to

42. RCIA, 128.

43. RCIA, 130.

> follow his commands; they have shared the company of their Christian brothers and sisters and joined with them in prayer.
>
> And so I announce to all of you here that our community has decided to call them to the sacraments. Therefore, I ask their godparents to state their opinion once again, so that all of you may hear.[44]

Addressing the godparents, the bishop continues: "As God is your witness, do you consider these candidates worthy to be admitted to the sacraments of Christian initiation?"[45] The godparents will hopefully testify positively to the bishop's question. This sort of questioning is purposely designed to "exclude any semblance of mere formality" and must be taken as a serious statement of the catechumens' preparedness. This is particularly made manifest when the bishop has not participated in an earlier deliberation (option B). In this case, he asks the godparents the following: "Have they faithfully listened to God's word proclaimed by the Church?" "Have they responded to that word and begun to walk in God's presence?" "Have they shared the company of their Christian brothers and sisters and

After the godparents have affirmed the catechumens' readiness to proceed to the sacraments of initiation, the catechumens' names are offered for enrollment.

44. RCIA, 131.

45. RCIA, 131.

joined with them in prayer?"[46] Once again, it is hopeful that the godparents will be able to authentically affirm the catechumens' wishes to proceed to the final turn of the journey to the Easter sacraments.

Immediately following the affirmation of the candidates by their sponsors and the entire Church, the bishop invites the catechumens to offer their names for enrollment.[47] He addresses the catechumens in these or similar words:

> And now, my dear catechumens, I address you. Your own godparents and teachers [and this entire community] have spoken in your favor. The Church in the name of Christ accepts their judgment and calls you to the Easter sacraments.
>
> Since you have already heard the call of Christ, you must now express your response to that call clearly and in the presence of the whole Church.
>
> Therefore, do you wish to enter fully into the life of the Church through the sacraments of baptism, confirmation, and the eucharist?[48]

After the bishop declares the catechumens members of the elect, he instructs the godparents to continue to care for them.

46. RCIA, 131.
47. RCIA, 132.
48. RCIA, 132.

The catechumens accept this invitation by responding "We do," and the bishop instructs them to offer their names for enrollment. "The candidates give their names, either going with their godparents to the celebrant or while remaining in place. The actual inscription of the names may be carried out in various ways. The candidates may inscribe their names themselves or they may call out their names, which are inscribed by the godparents or by the minister who presented the candidates."[49] Often the bishop is presented with the Book of the Elect from each parish community with the names of the catechumens previously inscribed.

After the enrollment of their names, the bishop declares the catechumens to be members of the elect. The bishop briefly explains the meaning of the enrollment of names and turns to the catechumens with these words: "I now declare you to be members of the elect, to be initiated into the sacred mysteries at the next Easter Vigil."[50] After the statement of praise by the newly elect—"Thanks be to God"—the bishop continues: "God is always faithful to those he calls: now it is your duty, as it is ours, both to be faithful to him in return and to strive courageously to reach the fullness of truth, which your election opens up before you."[51] The bishop concludes this act of admission into the elect by charging the godparents with the project of continuing to support the elect in their final weeks of preparation for Easter: "Godparents, you have spoken in favor of these catechumens: accept them now as chosen in the Lord and continue to sustain them through your loving care and example, until they come to share in the sacraments of God's life." Prior to the intercessions for the elect, the bishop invites the godparents to place a hand on the shoulder of the one for whom they have testified.

Receiving the elect with great joy, the assembly is invited to offer their prayer of intercession. If the Rite of Election takes place within a Mass, and the elect are to be dismissed prior to the Liturgy of the Eucharist, intercessions for the Church and the entire world are to be added to the prayers crafted for the elect. The bishop invites the community to prayer:

49. RCIA, 132.

50. RCIA, 133.

51. RCIA, 133.

> My brothers and sisters, in beginning this period of Lent, we look forward to celebrating at Easter the life-giving mysteries of our Lord's suffering, death, and resurrection. These elect, whom we bring with us to the Easter sacraments, will look to us for an example of Christian renewal. Let us pray to the Lord for them and for ourselves, that we may be renewed by one another's efforts and together come to share the joys of Easter.[52]

The RCIA provides two options for a set of intercessions to follow.[53] Several chosen from option B serve to demonstrate the overall intent of these intercessions: "That these elect may find joy in their daily prayer"; "That they may read your word and joyfully dwell on it in their hearts"; "That they may humbly acknowledge their faults and work wholeheartedly to correct them"; "That they may grow to love and seek virtue and holiness of life"; "That they may share with others the joy they have found in their faith."

The bishop concludes the intercessions for the elect with a special prayer of blessing. With his hands outstretched over the elect, he prays one of two prayers prescribed in the RCIA.[54] Both of them are worth contemplating.

Option A:

> Lord God,
> you created the human race
> and are the author of its renewal.
> Bless all your adopted children
> and add these chosen ones
> to the harvest of your new covenant.
>
> As true children of the promise,
> may they rejoice in eternal life,
> won, not by the power of nature,
> but through the mystery of your grace.
>
> We ask this through Christ our Lord.

52. RCIA, 134.
53. RCIA, 134.
54. RCIA, 135.

Option B:

Father of love and power,
it is your will to establish everything in Christ
and to draw us into his all-embracing love.

Guide the elect of your Church:
strengthen them in their vocation,
build them into the kingdom of your Son,
and seal them with the Spirit of your promise.

We ask this through Christ our Lord.

Both prayers are constructed to remind the elect that, while chosen by God, their call to conversion is ongoing. They are to recognize that the work being done in them is not of their own design ("the power of nature"), it is accomplished "through the mystery of your [God's] grace." For it is God who will "strengthen them," "build them," and "seal them."

The Rite of Election concludes with the dismissal of the elect (if the Eucharist is to be celebrated). If the rite takes place within the celebration of God's Word alone, the entire assembly is dismissed by the presider. When the elect are dismissed, the bishop may use the following formulary: "My dear elect, you have set out with us on the road that leads to the glory of Easter. Christ will be your way, your truth, and your life. Until we meet again for the scrutinies, walk always in his peace."[55] Those who have been welcomed more fully into the household of God by being named "elect" are now to demonstrate to the Church a fervent desire for purity of heart and knowledge of Christ, as they enter into a time of intense prayer and reflection.

55. RCIA, 136.

Chapter Five

Third Period / Third Step: Enlightenment and the Sacraments of Initiation

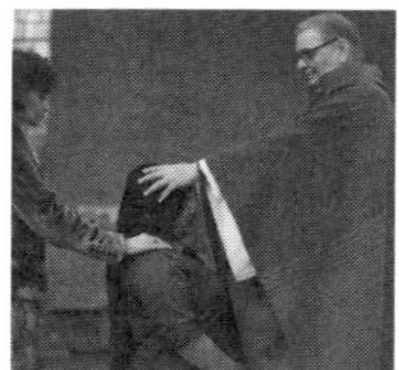

While Lent is understood to be the Church's period of preparation for the joy of Easter, the season was originally a time of purification for those awaiting Baptism. As infant Baptism came to replace adult initiation, the Lenten practices of fasting, almsgiving, and prayer were embraced by the already baptized. Unfortunately, what was lost in the transfer was the seriousness of the radical shift in allegiances demonstrated by the elect in the weeks immediately preceding Easter. Theodore of Mopsuestia, for example, describes the period of enlightenment as a sort of courtroom trial, with the candidate for Baptism as the defendant and the devil as the plaintiff:

> The candidate must then always have recourse to the "exorcists." You are, as it were, pleading a suit; you must stand in silence before your accuser. You stand with hands outstretched in the attitude of prayer and keep your eyes lowered. For the same reason you remove your outer garments and stand barefoot on sack-cloth.[1]

Although they had already handed in their names for Baptism and were chosen as the elect, those preparing for the Easter sacraments

1. Edward Yarnold, SJ, *The Awe-Inspiring Rites of Initiation: The Origins of the R.C.I.A.* 2nd ed. (Collegeville: Liturgical Press, 1994), 9–10.

were understood as being in a particularly vulnerable state, susceptible more than ever to the cunning of the Evil One. Similarly, Ambrose likens the final preparations of the elect to the grueling discipline of athletes:

> Can an athlete enjoy leisure once he has given in his name for an event? No, he trains and is anointed every day. He is given special food; discipline is imposed on him; he has to keep himself chaste. You too have given in your name for Christ's contest; you have entered for an event, and its prize is a crown. Practice, train, anoint yourself with the oil of gladness, an ointment that is never used up. Your food should be frugal, without intemperance or self-indulgence. Your drink should be more sparing for fear drunkenness should catch you unawares. Keep your body chaste so as to be fit to wear the crown. Otherwise your reputation may lose the favor of the spectators, and your supporters may see your negligence and abandon you. The Archangels, the Powers, the Dominions, the ten thousand times ten thousand Angels are all watching you. Before such spectators have some sense of shame and consider how dishonorable such conduct would be.[2]

Whether seen as a time to do battle with the devil or as a time to gain the strength and the agility of an athlete, Lent was designed as a time of serious purification of the heart and the soul, with changes affecting the body as well.

Although the RCIA makes room for the Period of Purification and Enlightenment to fall outside the season of Lent in rare, extraordinary circumstances, the rite envisions Lent as the context for final conversion:

> The period of purification and enlightenment, which the rite of election begins, customarily coincides with Lent. In the liturgy and liturgical catechesis of Lent the reminder of baptism already received or the preparation for its reception, as well as the theme of repentance, renew the entire community along with those being prepared to celebrate the paschal mystery in which each of the elect will share through the sacraments of initiation. For both the elect and the local community, therefore, the Lenten season is a time for spiritual recollection in preparation for the celebration of the paschal mystery.[3]

---

2. Ibid., 15.
3. RCIA, 138.

Clearly, the Rite of Christian Initiation of Adults, with its pattern of celebrating the scrutinies and the Presentations of the Creed and the Lord's Prayer during the liturgical framework of Lent, foresees the elect providing a ministry to the Church as a whole. As they kneel humbly before God, the Christian community and the presider ask God to "protect them from vain reliance on self and defend them from the power of Satan."[4] They selflessly demonstrate the dependence upon the Father's mercy that all Christians are to exemplify.

Period of Purification and Enlightenment

Every rite of passage involves letting go of some former way of life. When a driver's license is received at the age of sixteen, the expectation is that adolescence is let go for adult responsibility. This passage in life, however, involves little surrender to the past. The seriousness of baptismal commitment, on the other hand, requires a powerful and concentrated purification of life:

> This is a period of more intense spiritual preparation, consisting more in interior reflection than in catechetical instruction, and is intended to purify the minds and hearts of the elect as they search their own consciences and do penance. This period is intended as well to enlighten the minds and hearts of the elect with a deeper knowledge of Christ the Savior. The celebration of certain rites, particularly the scrutinies and the presentations, brings about this process of purification and enlightenment and extends it over the course of the entire Lenten season.[5]

Because the priest presides over the scrutinies in the context of the Sunday assembly and may preside over the Presentations of the Creed and of the Lord's Prayer as well, his presence in the Period of Purification and Enlightenment is to be particularly evident. The pastor empathizes fully with the elect during these final days of preparation. He may also be called upon to celebrate the "proximate preparation" with the elect on Holy Saturday as they await Baptism.[6]

The scrutiny rites that take place on the Third, Fourth, and Fifth Sundays of Lent most clearly demonstrate the life change that is placed before the elect as they prepare to join Christ's Body by

4. RCIA, 154, Option A.
5. RCIA, 139.
6. RCIA, 140.

liturgically celebrating the power of God to cast out sin and evil from the human heart. The RCIA offers the following description of the scrutinies:

> The scrutinies, which are solemnly celebrated on Sundays and are reinforced by an exorcism, are rites for self-searching and repentance and have above all a spiritual purpose. The scrutinies are meant to uncover, then heal all that is weak, defective, or sinful in the hearts of the elect; to bring out, then strengthen all that is upright, strong, and good. For the scrutinies are celebrated in order to deliver the elect from the power of sin and Satan, to protect them against temptation, and to give them strength in Christ, who is the way, the truth, and the life.[7]

Thus, the scrutinies are intended to publicly "complete the conversion of the elect and deepen their resolve to hold fast to Christ and to carry out their decision to love God above all."[8] They are celebrated in the Sunday assembly because the scrutinies serve to call the already baptized to ongoing conversion, leading them to celebrate the Sacrament of Reconciliation. The RCIA, therefore, commissions the priest or the deacon who presides over the scrutinies to "carry out the celebration in such a way that the faithful in the assembly will also derive benefit from the liturgy of the scrutinies and join in the intercessions for the elect."[9]

Furthermore, the scrutinies are intended not only to root out sin in the lives of the elect, but they are designed to enflame their spirits with the presence of Christ the Savior, "who is the living water (gospel of the Samaritan woman in the first scrutiny), the light of the world (gospel of the man born blind in the second scrutiny), the resurrection and the life (gospel of Lazarus in the third scrutiny)."[10] In the celebration of these three liturgical rites, the elect are to "receive new strength in the midst of their spiritual journey and they open their hearts to receive the gifts of the Savior."[11] The celebrations of the scrutinies are for the unbaptized; they are not to include the already baptized who may be preparing to be received into the

---

7. RCIA, 141.
8. RCIA, 141.
9. RCIA, 145.
10. RCIA, 143.
11. RCIA, 144.

Catholic Church or who may be completing their initiation with the sacraments of Confirmation and Eucharist.

In celebrating the scrutinies, the pastor is advised to prepare prayerfully and thoughtfully the three ritual Masses, "2. For the Celebration of the Scrutinies" which are composed for this time of enlightenment. Also, it is strongly recommended that the readings from the *Lectionary for Mass*, Year A, be proclaimed during the scrutiny Masses. If pastoral reasons dictate that the scrutinies cannot be celebrated on the Third, Fourth, and Fifth Sundays of Lent, "they are celebrated on other Sundays of Lent or even convenient days during the week."[12] Furthermore, if pastoral circumstances demand that the Period of Purification and Enlightenment occurs outside of Lent, the scrutinies are still to be celebrated on Sundays or weekdays, with the duration of a week between.[13] It is also necessary that the order of the Ritual Masses provided in "Christian Initiation: The Scrutinies" be followed, with the Mass with the Gospel of the Samaritan woman first, the Mass with the Gospel of the man born blind second, and the Mass with the Gospel of Lazarus third.[14]

Familiarity with the overall structure of the scrutinies will help the pastor lead the elect and the faithful to a profound awareness of the damaging effects of sin and the power of God's mercy. Because the scrutinies flow from the proclamation of the Gospel, a homily that prepares for the celebration of the particular scrutiny will prove helpful to the entire community. Regarding the nature of the homily, the RCIA offers this instruction: "After the readings and guided by them, the celebrant explains in the homily the meaning of the first [second or third] scrutiny in the light of the Lenten liturgy and of the spiritual journey of the elect."[15] Thus, a clear understanding of the scrutinies is demanded for the one who preaches on these Sundays.

12. RCIA, 146.
13. RCIA, 146.
14. RCIA, 146.
15. RCIA, 151.

The structure of the rite for the scrutinies is as follows:

Liturgy of the Word

- Readings
- Homily
- Invitation to Silent Prayer
- Intercessions for the Elect
- Exorcism
- Dismissal of the Elect

Liturgy of the Eucharist

The scrutinies are intended to enflame the elect with the presence of Christ.

After the homily, the elect and their godparents assemble before the presider. As in the Rite of Sending, it may be best for the elect to face the assembly, with the presider standing in the midst of the faithful. The presider first turns to the assembly and asks them to pray for the elect, that they "will be given a spirit of repentance, a sense of sin, and the true freedom of the children of God."[16] He then turns to the elect and invites them to pray in silence with

16. RCIA, 152.

these or similar words: “Elect of God, bow your heads [kneel down] and pray.”[17]

After a period of silence, everyone, including the elect with the right hand of their godparents placed on their shoulders, stand for the praying of intercessions specifically for the intention of the elect. If the elect are to be dismissed and the Eucharist to continue as usual, intentions other than those for the elect may be added to the given formulary.[18] A sampling of the prayers written for the First Scrutiny shows that the prayers are insightful in their depiction of God’s mercy and grace: “that they may ponder the word of God in their hearts and savor its meaning more fully day by day”; “that they may learn to know Christ, who came to save what was lost”; “that they may humbly confess themselves to be sinners”; “that they may sincerely reject everything in their lives that is displeasing and contrary to Christ.”[19] It is important to note that these intercessions include prayers for the entire Body of Christ, into whom the elect will be knitted as one: “that we ourselves in preparation for the Easter feast may seek a change of heart, give ourselves to prayer, and persevere in our good works”; “that throughout the whole world whatever is weak may be strengthened, whatever is broken restored, whatever is lost found, and what is found redeemed.” The intercessions clarify our need for conversion and ongoing transformation within the context of a world that can easily lose its way.

A prayer of exorcism serves as the conclusion to the intercessions for the elect. The presider faces the elect, and with hands joined, addresses God the Father and asks that he “protect them from vain reliance on self and defend them from the power of Satan.”[20] He continues pleading God the Father:

> Free them from the spirit of deceit,
> so that, admitting the wrong they have done,
> they may attain purity of heart
> and advance on the way to salvation.[21]

---

17. RCIA, 152.

18. RCIA, 153.

19. RCIA, 153.

20. RCIA, 154.

21. RCIA, 154.

This plea to the Father's grace concludes with the laying on of hands, which entails the presider laying hands on each of the elect "if this can be done conveniently."[22] The importance of laying hands on each of the elect should not be undervalued. The elect are in an extremely vulnerable state at this moment, and the power of touch should not be denied them.

After the laying of hands, the presider stretches out his hands over the elect and addresses the Lord Jesus, who is implored to strengthen the elect with his power and presence. The following prayer (option B) from the First Scrutiny embodies this request:

> Lord Jesus,
> in your merciful wisdom
> you touched the heart of the sinful woman
> and taught her to worship the Father
> in spirit and in truth.
>
> Now, by your power,
> free these elect from the cunning of Satan,
> as they draw near to the fountain of living water.
>
> Touch their hearts with the power of the Holy Spirit,
> that they may come to know the Father
> in true faith, which expresses itself in love,
> for you live and reign for ever and ever.[23]

Notice that the Triune God has been addressed in the two prayers. Not only is the Lord Jesus called upon to free the elect from sin and evil, but the Church prays that the Holy Spirit may come to increase the gifts of knowledge, faith, and love. To conclude the exorcism, the rite suggests the singing of an appropriate song that expresses the praise of the worshipping assembly for the bounty of mercy bestowed upon the Church in the scrutiny.

The scrutiny concludes with the dismissal of the elect:

> My dear friends, this community now sends you forth to reflect more deeply upon the word of God which you have shared with us today. Be assured of our loving support and prayers for you. We look forward to the day when you will share fully in the Lord's Table.[24]

---

22. RCIA, 154.
23. RCIA, 154.
24. RCIA, 155.

This simple dismissal concludes the ritual. The presider embodies sensitivity and warmth for the elect, whose need for forgiveness is acknowledged. They are to be freed from sin to be made ready for their full participation in Christ. As the RCIA contends, "The scrutinies are meant to uncover, then heal all that is weak, defective, or sinful in the hearts of the elect; to bring out, then strengthen all that is upright, strong, and good."[25] For this to happen most effectively, a relationship of empathy and understanding ought to exist between the pastor and the elect. He will hopefully have personal knowledge of both their weaknesses and strengths.

During this period, the Church also celebrates two important presentations—the Presentation of the Creed and the Presentation of the Lord's Prayer—which are made "in order to enlighten the elect."[26] Regarding the significance of what the Church intends to hand over to the elect, the RCIA instructs: "The Creed, as it recalls the wonderful deeds of God for the salvation of the human race, suffuses the vision of the elect with the sure light of faith. The Lord's Prayer fills them with a deeper realization of the new spirit of adoption by which they will call God their Father, especially in the midst of the eucharistic assembly."[27] This ritual handing over is designed so that the elect grow in their confident participation within the ambit of the praying Church; they are to experience a deepened oneness with the already baptized.

The RCIA directs that the first presentation be celebrated during the week following the First Scrutiny[28] and the second presentation during the week following the Third Scrutiny.[29] In other words, there is to be a spiritual connection here: the prayers of the scrutinies free the elect from the ways of sin so the elect might receive the prayers of the presentations and utter them in true faith. The elect "commit the Creed to memory" and "recite it publicly"[30] prior to their Baptism at the Easter Vigil.[31] Likewise, the Lord's

25. RCIA, 141.
26. RCIA, 147.
27. RCIA, 147.
28. RCIA, 148.
29. RCIA, 149.
30. RCIA, 148.
31. RCIA, 149.

Prayer is given to the elect to memorize as a sign of their full participation in the Eucharistic celebration: "When the elect have been baptized and take part in their first celebration of the eucharist, they will join the rest of the faithful in saying the Lord's Prayer."[32]

Ideally, the Presentations of the Creed and of the Lord's Prayer are to take place within Mass, "in the presence of a community of the faithful."[33] However, they may instead take place within a celebration of the Word of God. In this case, it is pastorally appropriate to invite the community to participate, as the wider parish community will not fully benefit from these important rites if they are celebrated only with the elect. The RCIA allows, for pastoral reasons, for the presentations to be celebrated at an earlier point within the catechumenate (see paragraphs 104 and 105); however, this is to be based on the fact that "the catechumens are judged ready for these celebrations."[34] Even outside the Period of Purification and Enlightenment, the presentations are to involve the parish community as a whole. An exploration of both presentations will help to demonstrate the gift both bestowed and received by the Church as it beholds the budding faith of the elect.

As stated earlier, the Presentation of the Creed is best celebrated during the week after the First Scrutiny.[35] The readings for the Liturgy of the Word are to be found in the *Lectionary for Mass* under the heading "Christian Initiation: Presentation of the Creed." With the Gospel text coming either from Matthew 16:13–18 ("On this rock I will build my Church") or John 12:44–50 ("I, the light, have come into the world, so that whoever believes in me need not remain in the dark any more"), the presider is to give a homily that explains "the meaning and importance of the Creed in relation to the teaching that the elect have already received and to the profession of faith that they must make at their baptism and uphold throughout their lives."[36] Once again, it is an important aspect of the ministry of the presider that this homily be thoughtfully and prayerfully prepared in advance of the celebration.

32. RCIA, 149.

33. RCIA, 157 and 178.

34. RCIA, 104.

35. RCIA, 157.

36. RCIA, 159.

After the homily, the elect are invited forward to receive the Creed.[37] They may either receive the Apostles' Creed (option A) or the Nicene Creed (option B). Although the Nicene Creed (also called the Niceno-Constantinopolitan Creed) is more regularly used in the Sunday assembly, the Apostles' Creed is more ancient and is directly tied to the baptismal liturgy. Regardless of the Creed chosen, it will be the duty of the elect to memorize the Creed and to recite it back to the Church in the preparation rites of Holy Saturday. Although the RCIA does not suggest that the Creed be handed over to the elect in a written format, the project of memorizing this formula in a few short weeks might be enhanced by afterwards providing the elect with copies of the Creed that correspond to the translation used in the liturgy. Before the presider orally presents the words of the chosen Creed, he addresses the elect in these or similar words: "My dear friends, listen carefully to the words of that faith by which you will be justified. The words are few, but the mysteries they contain are great. Receive them with a sincere heart and be faithful to them."[38] He begins the Creed, with the assembly joining in the profession.

The elect listen to the faith of the Church and make no verbal response to the reception of the Creed. Their *reditio*, or handing back, of the Creed will take place during the Preparation Rites on Holy Saturday. The presider concludes the profession of the Creed by inviting the assembly to pray for the elect "that God in his mercy may make them responsive to his love, so that through the waters of rebirth they may receive pardon for their sins and have life in Christ Jesus our Lord."[39] Allowing the assembly a time of silence for prayer, the presider then stretches his hands over the elect and prays:

Lord,
eternal source of light, justice, and truth,
take under your tender care
your servants N. and N.

Purify them and make them holy;
give them true knowledge, sure hope, and sound understanding,
and make them worthy
to receive the grace of baptism.

37. RCIA, 160.
38. RCIA, 160.
39. RCIA, 161.

We ask this through Christ our Lord.[40]

In keeping with the general purpose of this final period prior to the celebration of the Easter sacraments, this prayer fittingly asks the Lord to "purify" the elect and to give them "true knowledge, sure hope, and sound understanding." If the presentation takes place within a Mass, the elect are dismissed at this point; otherwise, the entire gathering is dismissed in peace.

As stated earlier, the Presentation of the Lord's Prayer is generally celebrated during the week after the Third Scrutiny. The readings for the Liturgy of the Word are to be found in the *Lectionary for Mass* under the heading "Christian Initiation: Presentation of the Lord's Prayer." Immediately prior to the proclamation of the Gospel, the deacon or another minister invites the elect to come forward. The presider addresses the elect, inviting them to listen carefully to the Gospel text from Matthew in which Jesus teaches his disciples to pray. The proclamation of this Gospel text serves as the Presentation of the Lord's Prayer to the elect. Then, in the course of his homily, the presider "explains the meaning and importance of the Lord's Prayer."[41] The homilist is charged with the difficult duty of explaining the nature of the Lord's Prayer—difficult because it is so frequently recited, in such a wide range of settings, and can be often prayed with little thought. For this reason, it would be helpful for the priest to visit with the elect prior to this celebration and invite them to reflect upon the meaning of the words of the Lord's Prayer in their lives. The priest might ask them to comment on the words or phrases in the prayer that are foreign to them. That information should help him prepare a homily that will enlighten the elect.

After the homily, the presider invites the faithful in the same words as at the Presentation of the Creed: "Let us pray for these elect, that God in his mercy may make them responsive to his love, so that through the waters of rebirth they may receive pardon for their sins and have life in Christ Jesus our Lord."[42] After a period of silent prayer, the presider stretches his hands over the elect and prays:

40. RCIA, 161.

41. RCIA, 181.

42. RCIA, 182.

Almighty and eternal God,
you continually enlarge the family of your Church.

Deepen the faith and understanding
of these elect, chosen for baptism.
Give them new birth in your living waters,
so that they may be numbered among your adopted children.

We ask this through Christ our Lord.[43]

As in the prayer over the elect at the Presentation of the Creed, this prayer seeks the enlightenment of the elect as they prepare for Baptism. If the presentation takes place within a Mass, the elect are dismissed at this point; otherwise, the entire gathering is dismissed in peace.

The final liturgical events that ought to include the parish priest are the Preparation Rites on Holy Saturday. Holy Saturday is a day of frenzied activity. Many last-minute details are attended to in readying the worship space for the Easter Vigil, while many families are busy readying their homes for Easter feasts. The Church asks the elect to prepare themselves spiritually on this day in a special way. Despite all of the added parish responsibilities that will occupy his time on Holy Saturday, the pastor is invited to shepherd the elect with special care.

The RCIA calls the elect to spiritual and bodily discipline on this day: "The elect are to be advised that on Holy Saturday they should refrain from their usual activities, spend their time in prayer and reflection, and, as far as they can, observe a fast."[44] Even though the elect, having journeyed with the parish during its forty-day fast, know the difficulties of restricting their food intake, they must be assisted to apply this fast to their coming immersion into Christ. In other words, those responsible for their formation must help the elect understand the nature of their sacrifice, namely, that which allows them to yearn and hunger ever more deeply for union with Christ. The pastor may assist in these moments of final preparation by offering to the elect a personal testimony on the beauty of the Easter Vigil and perhaps a reflection on how to reverently receive the Body and Blood of Christ. He may furthermore wish to offer words

43. RCIA, 182.
44. RCIA, 185 §1.

that alleviate the anxiety that many of the elect will surely have of being on public display at the Vigil. Nevertheless, the RCIA envisions Holy Saturday as a time that will draw the elect together "for reflection and prayer" and for the celebration of other rites that will focus their attention on the Lord and his Paschal Mystery.[45]

The liturgical rites that may be celebrated on Holy Saturday are the Presentation of the Lord's Prayer, if it has been deferred, the Recitation of the Creed, the Ephphetha Rite, and the Choosing of a Baptismal Name and Concluding Rites. Choosing which rites to celebrate and establishing the order of their celebration is a matter of pastoral need, considering what will be most beneficial to the elect. However, the RCIA instructs that if the Creed has not formally been presented in a liturgical fashion, then its recitation should not be celebrated.[46] Furthermore, when both the Recitation of the Creed and the Ephphetha Rite are celebrated, the ephphetha ritual takes place within the context of the former liturgy and is positioned immediately before the "Prayer before the Recitation."[47] An overview of these preparatory celebrations will help the pastor determine which rites are appropriate for the circumstances of the elect.

First, the Recitation of the Creed may take place on Holy Saturday if the Presentation of the Creed was celebrated previously. This liturgy celebrates the returning of the Creed by the elect, who have put it to memory and now confidently proclaim it in anticipation of making baptismal vows in the coming hours. The RCIA states: "The rite of recitation of the Creed prepares the elect for the profession of faith they will make immediately before they are baptized; the rite also instructs them in their duty to proclaim the message of the Gospel."[48] It begins with a reading of either Matthew 16:13–17 ("You are Christ, the Son of the living God") or John 6:35, 63–71 ("To whom shall we go? You have the words of eternal life"), which is followed by a brief homily. Both of these passages deal with the proclamation of faith. The homilist may wish to ask the elect to consider how they are invited to make their lives a bold proclamation of faith. How has their growth into Christ throughout their

45. RCIA, 185 §2.

46. RCIA, 186 §1.

47. RCIA, 186 §2.

48. RCIA, 193.

participation in the Christian initiation process led them to a deeper understanding of his name?

After the homily, the presider utters a prayer for the elect before they recite the Creed. If the Ephphetha Rite is to be celebrated on this day, it is inserted into the liturgy at this point. With outstretched hands, the presider prays:

> Lord,
> we pray to you for these elect,
> who have now accepted for themselves
> the loving purpose and the mysteries
> that you revealed in the life of your Son.
>
> As they profess their belief with their lips,
> may they have faith in their hearts
> and accomplish your will in their lives.
>
> We ask this through Christ our Lord.[49]

At the conclusion of this prayer, the elect are invited to recite either the Apostles' Creed or the Nicene Creed, whichever one they were earlier presented.[50] At least a representation of the parish should attend this liturgy, as it is the Church as a whole who is "receiving back" the proclamation of faith made by the elect. The recitation of the Creed serves as the climax of the liturgy; the rite has no closing prayer, final blessing, or dismissal.

A second liturgical rite that takes place on Holy Saturday is the Ephphetha Rite. The word *ephphetha* is a command word that means "be opened" and comes from the encounter between Jesus and a man who could neither hear nor speak (Mark 7). This is a beautiful and yet so very simple ritual that will take only a few moments of the pastor's time. The RCIA states, "By the power of its symbolism the ephphetha rite, or rite of opening the ears and mouth, impresses on the elect their need of grace in order that they may hear the word of God and profess it for their salvation."[51] If it stands on its own and is not celebrated within the liturgy of the Recitation of the Creed, the Ephphetha Rite begins with the reading of Mark 7:31–37 ("Ephphetha, that is, be opened.") together with a "brief

49. RCIA, 195.

50. RCIA, 196.

51. RCIA, 197.

explanation" of the passage.[52] The one explaining this Gospel text should not approach the task lightly. It is no easy task "to hear" the

The words of the ephphetha stand alone as a profound encounter with the Lord's healing touch.

Word of God in our world or "to speak" it with conviction. The homilist may want to ask the elect to consider how they hear things differently now that they have encountered Christ. Has the content of their speech changed in the months since embarking on the journey to Christian initiation?

After the reading and instruction, the elect stand in front of the celebrant.[53] If this liturgy is celebrated in a circle, the presider may consider moving from person to person, rather than the elect approaching him individually. The instructions suggest that a song may accompany the ritual gesture of the ephphetha.[54] Whether accompanied by song or silence, the presider touches the right and left ear and the closed lips of each of the elect and states: "Ephphetha: that is, be opened, that you may profess the faith you hear, to the

52. RCIA, 198.

53. RCIA, 199.

54. RCIA, 199.

praise and the glory of God." Nothing more constitutes this liturgical rite; the words and actions of the ephphetha are meant to stand alone as a profound encounter with the Lord's healing touch.

Another preparation rite to strengthen the elect for the celebration of the initiation at Easter is a very simple ritual called Choosing a Baptismal Name. While this rite is intended for execution on Holy Saturday (as well as within the Rite of Acceptance into the Order of Catechumens), it is not practiced in the United States:

> The National Conference of Catholic Bishops establishes as the norm in the dioceses of the United States that there is to be no giving of a new name. It also approves leaving to the discretion of the diocesan bishop the giving of a new name to persons from those cultures in which it is the practice of non-Christian religions to give a new name.[55]

While not customarily used, the purpose of this rite is theologically sound:

> The elect may choose a new name, which is either a traditional Christian name or a name of regional usage that is not incompatible with Christian beliefs. Whether it seems better suited to the circumstances and the elect are not too numerous, the naming may consist simply in an explanation of the name given each of the elect.[56]

Just as the naming of an infant at Baptism is to be understood as entrance into the Christian household, so too does the choosing of a baptismal name represent the desire to be recognized completely as a disciple. Nevertheless, the decision made to omit this rite within the United States represents pastoral care and respect for the human person whose conversion into Christ is not a total shedding of a previous life, but rather is growth, enlightenment, and expansion into a new world. One's name given at birth is to be sanctified.

The rite of choosing a baptismal name could easily be mistaken for the choosing of a Confirmation name, which continues to be a tradition in many places. It is simply an act of honoring one's name as belonging to Christ. If it is deemed pastorally appropriate to use this rite, the liturgy consists simply of a reading and instruction.[57] Suggested are the following readings: Genesis 17:1–7 ("You will

55. RCIA, 33 §4.

56. RCIA, 200.

57. RCIA, 201.

be called Abraham"), Isaiah 62:1–5 ("You will be called by a new name"), Revelation 3:11–13 ("I will write my new name upon him"), Matthew 16:13–18 ("You are Peter"), and John 1:40–42 ("You will be called Peter"). After the proclamation of one of these readings, the presider may then offer a brief explanation regarding the dignity of a name. Following the celebration of the Word, the names of the elect are honored by their stating either new names (option A) or by stating their given names (option B).[58] If the elect choose new names, the presider responds by stating: "N., from now on you will [also] be called N." The elect reply "Amen" or some other words of thanksgiving. If option B is used, and the elect state their given names, the presider "applies some Christian interpretation to the given name of each of the elect."[59] Other than the verbal approval given to their reception of a new name or to the Christianizing of their given name, there is no formal ending to this rite.

The final preparation rite is called simply Concluding Rites. This rite consists of a blessing prayer and a dismissal. Obviously, if this rite is to take place on Holy Saturday, it is to be reserved for the last moment of prayer before the elect disperse to ready themselves for the Vigil. The presider invites everyone to prayer and utters the following prayer with his hands outstretched over the elect:

> Father,
> through your holy prophets
> you proclaimed to all who draw near you,
> "Wash and be cleansed,"
> and through Christ you have granted us rebirth in the Spirit.
>
> Bless these your servants
> as they earnestly prepare for baptism.
>
> Fulfill your promise:
> sanctify them in preparation for your gifts,
> that they may come to be reborn as your children
> and enter the community of your Church.
>
> We ask this through Christ our Lord.[60]

58. RCIA, 202.
59. RCIA, 202.
60. RCIA, 204.

This prayer seeks God's guidance of the elect as they enter into the very personal preparation of the remaining hours before they are to be baptized. There may be moments of insecurity and doubt in their minds and hearts as they look forward to the Vigil, and this prayer is meant to give them peace and calm. The Lord's abiding presence with the elect is reinforced in the dismissal that concludes this rite: "May the Lord be with you until we gather again to celebrate his paschal mystery."[61] The elect respond "Amen" and depart.

Pastoral Note on Anointing on Holy Saturday

The third edition of *The Roman Missal* directs that "if the anointing of adults with the Oil of Catechumens has not taken place beforehand, as part of the immediately preparatory rites" it is to take place before the renunciation of Satan and the profession of faith at the Easter Vigil.[62] However, the bishops of the United States have determined that anointing with the Oil of Catechumens must occur during the catechumenate or within the Period of Purification and Enlightenment. The RCIA clearly states:

> The National Conference of Catholic Bishops approves the omission of the anointing with the oil of catechumens both in the celebration of baptism and in the optional preparation rites for Holy Saturday. Thus, anointing with the oil of catechumens is reserved for use in the period of the catechumenate and in the period of purification and enlightenment and is not to be included in the preparation rites on Holy Saturday or in the celebration of initiation at the Easter Vigil or at another time.[63]

Therefore, even though the third edition of *The Roman Missal* was published more recently than the Rite of Christian Initiation of Adults and represents the universal law of the Church, the adaptations approved by the conferences of bishops serve as particular law. Quite simply, anointing with oil is not used as a preparation ritual on Holy Saturday or as part of the Vigil.

61. RCIA, 204.

62. *The Roman Missal* (RM), Easter Vigil, 48.

63. RCIA, 33 §7.

Celebration of the Sacraments of Initiation

The third step, or time of ritual celebration marking the passage of the elect to the state of neophyte, is the celebration of the sacraments of initiation. During the Triduum the Church is immersed in rehearsing the attitudes contained in the Paschal Mystery: self-sacrifice, obedience, and willing surrender to God's will. How fitting that in the evening shadows of Holy Saturday the Church gathers to hear its primary stories of salvation history and to participate in the transition of the elect into fullness of life in the resurrected Lord:

> The third step in the Christian initiation of adults is the celebration of the sacraments of baptism, confirmation, and eucharist. Through this final step the elect, receiving pardon for their sins, are admitted into the people of God. They are graced with adoption as children of God and are led by the Holy Spirit into the promised fullness of time begun in Christ and, as they share in the eucharistic sacrifice and meal, even to a foretaste of the kingdom of God.[64]

The Easter Vigil, "the greatest and most noble of all solemnities,"[65] is so patterned to allow the entire Christian community to realize anew its journey of faith. Those who are led to the waters of Baptism provide a tangible sign of what takes place in each member of the Body of Christ as promises of Baptism are renewed and fidelity to the Kingdom is sealed in the sharing of Communion.

Preparing the Easter Vigil and ensuring that all of the ministries that undergird its performance is one of the chief duties of the pastor. First and foremost, he must provide for the spiritual welfare of the elect as they await Baptism. Although many last-minute details will undoubtedly cause distraction for the pastor in the time leading up to the lighting of the new fire and the blessing of the Paschal candle at the outset of the liturgy, he needs to be present to the community as it gathers by setting a tone that is welcoming and joyful. Since the RCIA instructs that "preferably the bishop himself presides as celebrant"[66] of the Easter Vigil, the local pastor needs to see himself, at this moment more than ever, as the bishop's delegate. For this reason, the more he can embody the care of a loving

64. RCIA, 206.

65. RM, Easter Vigil, 2.

66. RCIA, 207.

shepherd with a style of leadership that is humble and gracious, the more the elect and the entire community will be drawn into the mystery of paschal life—dying to self to live anew in Christ.

If there is reason for celebrating the sacraments of initiation at an occasion other than the Vigil (the Rite suggests that such a reason may be that a great number of people are to be baptized), the priest must carefully discern the time when the sacraments are to be celebrated. "When the celebration takes place outside the usual time, care should be taken to ensure that it has a markedly paschal character."[67] The rite offers the following instructions concerning moving the sacraments of initiation to a time other than the Vigil:

> Even when the usual time has otherwise been observed, it is permissible, but only for serious pastoral needs (for example, if there are a great many people to be baptized), to choose a day other than the Easter Vigil or Easter Sunday, but preferably one during the Easter season, to celebrate the sacraments of initiation. . . . When the time is changed in either way, even though the rite of Christian initiation occurs at a different point in the liturgical year, the structure of the entire rite, with its properly spaced intervals, remains the same.[68]

> As far as possible, the sacraments of initiation are to be celebrated on a Sunday, using, as occasion suggests, the Sunday Mass or one of the ritual Masses "Christian Initiation: Baptism."[69]

Thus, in the rare situation of celebrating the sacraments of initiation apart from the Easter Vigil, the pastor must resist the temptation to allow convenience to guide the scheduling of this step into the Christian faith. For example, if one of the elect were to become ill and unable to participate in the Vigil, the priest is not to celebrate the sacraments privately or in a manner that does not maintain the solemnity of the Easter Vigil. Instead, he must ensure that any cause for celebrating the sacraments of initiation at a time other than the Vigil leads to a liturgy that contains a "markedly paschal character" and thus the dignity and beauty of Easter.

In addition to establishing the tone for the celebration of the Vigil, the priest also should demonstrate great concern for the

67. RCIA, 208.

68. RCIA, 26.

69. RCIA, 27.

Regard should be shown for the symbols of Baptism.

quality of the symbols used in the celebration of the sacraments of initiation. Several of the primary symbols are mentioned in the following rubric on the celebration of Baptism:

> The celebration of baptism has as its center and high point the baptismal washing and the invocation of the Holy Trinity. Beforehand there are rites that have an inherent relationship to the baptismal washing: first, the blessing of water, then the renunciation of sin by the elect, and their profession of faith. Following the baptismal washing, the effects received through this sacrament are given expression in the explanatory rites: the anointing with chrism (when confirmation does not immediately follow baptism), the clothing with a white garment, and the presentation of a lighted candle.[70]

Clearly, concern for the quality of the "baptismal washing" is preeminent among all the initiation symbols. The priest ought to consider it his responsibility to ensure that the following requirements concerning the water and the font, found in Christian Initiation, General Introduction, are met:

70. RCIA, 209.

> The water used in baptism should be true water and, both for the sake of authentic sacramental symbolism and for hygienic reasons, should be pure and clean.[71]
>
> The baptismal font, or the vessel in which on occasion the water is prepared for celebration of the sacrament in the sanctuary, should be spotlessly clean and of pleasing design.[72]
>
> If the climate requires, provision should be made for the water to be heated beforehand.[73]
>
> The baptistery or the area where the baptismal font is located should be reserved for the sacrament of baptism and should be worthy to serve as the place where Christians are reborn in water and the Holy Spirit. The baptistery may be situated in a chapel either inside or outside the church or in some other part of the church easily seen by the faithful; it should be large enough to accommodate a good number of people.[74]

Furthermore, from the introduction to the third step found in the RCIA:

> In the celebration of baptism the washing with water should take on its full importance as the sign of that mystical sharing in Christ's death and resurrection through which those who believe in his name die to sin and rise to eternal life. Either immersion or the pouring of water should be chosen for the rite, whichever will serve in individual cases and in the various traditions and circumstances to ensure the clear understanding that this washing is not a mere purification rite but the sacrament of being joined to Christ.[75]

Thus, the pastor, who "stirs up the waters," might consider the construction of a pool with running water that allows for the celebration of Baptism by immersion. The water used at Baptism is meant to convey the multifold imagery contained in the blessing of water: the waters that were breathed upon by the Spirit "in the first moments of the world's creation," the waters upon which Noah traveled for "an end to vice and a beginning of virtue," the waters of the Red Sea by which God set Israel "free from slavery to Pharaoh,"

71. CI, 18.
72. CI, 19.
73. CI, 20.
74. CI, 25.
75. RCIA, 213.

the waters of the Jordan in which Jesus "was baptized by John" and "anointed with the Holy Spirit," and the waters that mingled with the Lord's blood "as he hung upon the Cross."[76] Concern for the water of the font encapsulates the overall concern that the pastor is to have for the very nature of the material used for symbols of initiation as well as the way in which they are allowed to unfold with grace and abundance.

Yet another responsibility of the pastor during the preparation of the Easter Vigil concerns the liturgical texts themselves. The *Roman Missal* contains all of the texts that are used in the Vigil, with the exception of the rites of Baptism and Confirmation, which can be accessed in the *Rite of Christian Initiation of Adults*. It is especially important that the priest use the texts of the Missal, as in some cases, the language differs. Some parishes will make the decision to place a set of liturgical texts in a separate presider's binder. If this is a pastor's preference, great care must be taken to follow the ritual as prescribed. The tendency to take shortcuts is often the outcome of reproducing liturgical texts (not to mention that ritual elements may get shifted around without clear theological or pastoral reasoning).

Over and above all of his duties with regard to preparing for the Easter Vigil, the pastor must have a thorough understanding of the celebration as a whole. He needs to appreciate the symbolism of the Easter fire and the importance of gathering the community around it. He must have a genuine appreciation for the nature of the Liturgy of the Word on this night of nights, when the Church contemplates the way God desires to save his people in every age. He ought to comprehend the way the Easter Vigil flows seamlessly from the celebration of the Lord's Supper on Holy Thursday and the Adoration of the Cross on Good Friday as well as the way it opens the doors to the joy of Easter Sunday and the fifty days of feasting. Finally, the presider has the duty of understanding why the celebration of the sacraments of initiation unfolds as it does. For that reason, the ritual components of the Vigil will be examined in the pages ahead.

76. RM, Easter Vigil, 44.

The structure of the Easter Vigil and the Celebration of the Sacraments of Initiation is as follows:

Service of Light

Liturgy of the Word

Celebration of Baptism
- Presentation of the Candidates
- Invitation to Prayer
- Litany of the Saints
- Prayer over the Water
- Profession of Faith
    - Renunciation of Sin
    - Profession of Faith
- Baptism
- Explanatory Rites
    - Clothing with a Baptismal Garment (optional)
    - Presentation of a Lighted Candle

Celebration of Confirmation
- Invitation
- Laying on of Hands
- Anointing with Chrism

Renewal of Baptismal Promises
- Invitation
- Renewal of Baptismal Promises
    - Renunciation of Sin
    - Profession of Faith
- Sprinkling with Baptismal Water

Liturgy of the Eucharist

Like our ancestors in the desert, who followed a pillar of cloud by day and a pillar of fire by night, the solemn commemoration of Christian liberation opens around "a blazing fire"[77] that provides the light of guidance by which the Church will proclaim the wonders

77. RM, 8.

of this night. The priest's greeting at the opening of the service of light sets the stage:

> Dear brethren (brothers and sisters),
> on this most sacred night,
> in which our Lord Jesus Christ
> passed over from death to life,
> the Church calls upon her sons and daughters,
> scattered throughout the world,
> to come together to watch and pray.
> If we keep the memorial
> of the Lord's paschal solemnity in this way,
> listening to his word and celebrating his mysteries,
> then we shall have the sure hope
> of sharing his triumph over death
> and living with him in God.[78]

The action of watching and praying in the evening hours embodies true hopefulness. The presider turns to the fire, blesses it, and proceeds to mark the Paschal candle with the signs of Christ's cosmic dominion: "Christ yesterday and today, / the Beginning and the End, / the Alpha / and the Omega. / All time belongs to him / and all the ages. / To him be glory and power / through every age and for ever. Amen."[79] The candle and its light symbolize the total victory of Christ's Resurrection, namely, that nothing is left untouched by his love. The priest lights the Paschal candle and announces: "May the light of Christ rising in glory dispel the darkness of our hearts and minds."[80] Thanking God for the marvelous Light of Christ, the faithful enter the darkened church and assemble for the Easter Proclamation (the *Exsultet*). With the lights of the worship space fully illuminated,[81] the Church proclaims its great joy: "Rejoice, let Mother Church also rejoice, arrayed with the lightning of his glory let this holy building shake with joy, filled with the mighty voices of the people."[82]

78. RM, Easter Vigil, 9.
79. RM, Easter Vigil, 11.
80. RM, Easter Vigil, 14.
81. RM, Easter Vigil, 17.
82. RM, Easter Vigil, 19.

The Liturgy of the Word constitutes the second major component of the Easter Vigil. "In this Vigil, the mother of all Vigils, nine readings are provided, seven from the Old Testament and two from the New (the Epistle and Gospel), all of which should be read whenever this can be done, so that the character of the Vigil, which demands an extended period of time, may be preserved."[83] To reduce the number of readings undermines the overall schema of immersing the Christian community into the entirety of God's plan of salvation. From the moment creation came into being, with God stamping living and inanimate creatures with his approval, through the coming of his Son into the world and the establishment of the Church, God's desire to redeem is a mystery that demands contemplation. The presider invites the assembly to participate in the Liturgy of the Word with these or similar words:

> Dear brethren (brothers and sisters),
> now that we have begun our solemn Vigil,
> let us listen with quiet hearts to the Word of God.
> Let us meditate on how God in times past saved his people
> and in these, the last days, has sent us his Son as our Redeemer.
> Let us pray that our God may complete this paschal work of salvation
> by the fullness of redemption.[84]

Concluding each of the Old Testament readings with an accompanying Responsorial Psalm and a prayer, the Church listens to stories from Genesis 1:1—2:2 (on creation), Genesis 22:1–18 (on Abraham's sacrifice), Exodus 14:15—15:1 (on the passage through the Red Sea), Isaiah 54:5–14 (on the new Jerusalem), Isaiah 55:1–11 (on salvation freely offered to all), Baruch 3:9–15, 31—4:4 (on the fountain of wisdom), and Ezekiel 36:16–28 (on a new heart and a new spirit).[85]

The seven readings from the Old Testament, which survey salvation history, allow the Church to herald the coming of Christ and the praise of God's name. "After the last reading from the Old Testament with its Responsorial Psalm and its prayer, the altar candles are lit, and the Priest intones the hymn Gloria in excelsis Deo (Glory to God in the highest), which is taken up by all, while

83. RM, Easter Vigil, 20.

84. RM, Easter Vigil, 22.

85. See RM, Easter Vigil, 24, 25, 26, 27, 28, 29, and 30.

bells are rung, according to local custom."[86] At the conclusion of the Gloria, the presider prays the following Collect:

> O God, who make this most sacred night radiant
> with the glory of the Lord's Resurrection,
> stir up in your Church a spirit of adoption,
> so that, renewed in body and mind,
> we may render you undivided service.
> Through our Lord Jesus Christ, your Son,
> who lives and reigns with you in the unity of the Holy Spirit,
> one God, for ever and ever.[87]

Soon the assembly will gather around the waters of Baptism and witness God's fatherly love in response to the Church's plea: "stir up in your Church a spirit of adoption." First, however, all listen attentively to Paul's Letter to the Romans (6:3–11): "Brothers and sisters: Are you unaware that we who were baptized into Christ Jesus were baptized into his death? . . . If, then, we have died with Christ, we believe that we shall also live with him."[88] Life with Christ is the prize of those willing to die to self. With renewed joy at the life-giving prospects of faith, the Church sings its "Alleluia" and listens to the Gospel of Jesus' empty tomb (Year A—Matthew 28:1–10; Year B—Mark 16:1–7; Year C—Luke 24:1–12).[89] The homily, "even if brief, is not to be omitted"[90] and should link the hearing of the Word to the baptismal liturgy that follows.

In moving from the Liturgy of the Word to the celebration of Baptism, it should be noted that the RCIA requires that Baptism be celebrated "in view of the faithful."[91] If the baptismal font is located in a chapel apart from the main body of the assembly, the RCIA directs that the Baptisms take place "in the sanctuary, where a vessel of water for the rite should be prepared beforehand."[92] The Presentation of the Candidates will unfold according to the placement of the font, with three options offered in the Rite.[93] Option A is

86. RM, Easter Vigil, 31.
87. RM, Easter Vigil, 32.
88. *Lectionary for Mass*, 41.
89. *Lectionary for Mass*, 41.
90. RM, Easter Vigil, 36.
91. RCIA, 218.
92. RCIA, 218.
93. RCIA, 219.

to be used when Baptism is celebrated immediately at the baptismal font with no accompanying procession. Option B entails a procession to the font led by a minister carrying the Paschal candle, followed by those to be baptized and their godparents, with the assembly singing the Litany of the Saints. Option C is used when Baptism is celebrated in the sanctuary, with the elect and their godparents called forward. Either after the procession and the singing of the Litany (Option B) or after the candidates and their godparents have gathered (Options A and C), the presider invites the assembly to pray for those to be baptized in these or similar words:

> Dearly beloved,
> with one heart and one soul, let us by our prayers
> come to the aid of these our brothers and sisters in their blessed hope,
> so that, as they approach the font of rebirth,
> the almighty Father may bestow on them
> all his merciful help.[94]

If Option A or C is used, the Litany of the Saints takes place in response to this invitation; otherwise, the assembly prays in silence for several moments before the presider blesses the water.[95]

The blessing of the water is an ancient prayer that testifies to the Church's complete dependence upon the power of God to bring about new life. The RCIA states:

> The blessing thus introduces an invocation of the Trinity at the very outset of the celebration of baptism. For it calls to mind the mystery of God's love from the beginning of the world and the creation of the human race; by invoking the Holy Spirit and proclaiming Christ's death and resurrection, it impresses on the mind the newness of Christian baptism, by which we share in his own death and resurrection and receive the holiness of God himself.[96]

The presider at the baptismal liturgy would do well to meditate upon the Prayer over the Water:

> O God, who by invisible power
> accomplish a wondrous effect
> through sacramental signs

---

94. RM, Easter Vigil, 40.
95. RM, Easter Vigil, 41.
96. RCIA, 210.

and who in many ways have prepared water, your creation,
to show forth the grace of Baptism;

O God, whose Spirit
in the first moments of the world's creation
hovered over the waters,
so that the very substance of water
would even then take to itself the power to sanctify;

O God, who by the outpouring of the flood
foreshadowed regeneration,
so that from the mystery of one and the same element of water
would come an end to vice and a beginning of virtue;

O God, who caused the children of Abraham
to pass dry-shod through the Red Sea,
so that the chosen people,
set free from slavery to Pharaoh,
would prefigure the people of the baptized;

O God, whose Son,
baptized by John in the waters of the Jordan,
was anointed with the Holy Spirit,
and, as he hung upon the Cross,
gave forth water from his side along with blood,
and after his Resurrection, commanded his disciples:
"Go forth, teach all nations, baptizing them
in the name of the Father and of the Son and of the Holy Spirit,"
look now, we pray, upon the face of your Church
and graciously unseal for her the fountain of Baptism.

May this water receive by the Holy Spirit
the grace of your Only Begotten Son,
so that human nature, created in your image
and washed clean through the Sacrament of Baptism
from all the squalor of the life of old,
may be found worthy to rise to the life of newborn children
through water and the Holy Spirit.

At this point in the prayer, the presider may lower the Paschal candle either once or three times into the water as a sign of Christ's sanctifying and vivifying presence. He continues:

May the power of the Holy Spirit,
O Lord, we pray,
come down through your Son
into the fullness of this font,

The presider holds the candle in the water and continues:

so that all who have been buried with Christ
by Baptism into death
may rise again to life with him.
Who lives and reigns with you in the unity of the Holy Spirit,
one God, for ever and ever.[97]

As the candle is lifted out of the water, the people acclaim: "Springs of water, bless the Lord; praise and exalt him above all for ever."[98] It is important to note that, after the blessing of water, the Missal offers the following rubric: "If the anointing of the adults with the Oil of Catechumens has not taken place beforehand, as part of the immediately preparatory rites, it occurs at this moment."[99] However, as stated earlier, the bishops of the United States have mandated that anointing with the Oil of Catechumens not take place at the Vigil.

With the candidates for Baptism and their godparents gathered around the font, the presider continues with the profession of faith, which consists of both the renunciation of sin and the profession itself. While *The Roman Missal* permits a consolidation of the questions of those to be baptized and the renewal of baptismal promises,[100] it is most important to focus attention upon the profession of faith on the part of the elect. The RCIA states:

> In their renunciation of sin and profession of faith those to be baptized express their explicit faith in the paschal mystery that has already been recalled in the blessing of water and that will be connoted by the words of the sacrament soon to be spoken by the baptizing minister. Adults are not saved unless they come forward by their own accord and with the will to accept God's gift through their own belief. The faith of those to be baptized is not simply the faith of the Church, but the personal faith

97. RM, Easter Vigil, 46.

98. RM, Easter Vigil, 47.

99. RM, Easter Vigil, 48.

100. "Where many are to be baptized on this night, it is possible to arrange the rite so that, immediately after the response of those to be baptized and of the godparents and the parents, the Celebrant asks for and receives the renewal of baptismal promises of all present" (RM, Easter Vigil, 49).

> of each one of them and each of one of them is expected to keep it a living faith.[101]

Ideally, therefore, each candidate for Baptism is asked individually to reject sin and to profess the faith. However, if the number of those to be baptized prohibits this, they may be interrogated as a group and profess the faith as a group.[102] "Each candidate is baptized immediately after his or her profession of faith."[103]

The RCIA notes that adults may be baptized in one of two ways, either by immersion (Option A) or by the pouring of water (Option B). Rubrics govern carefully the manner of each. "If baptism is by immersion, of the whole body or of the head only, decency and decorum should be preserved. Either or both godparents touch the candidate. The celebrant, immersing the candidate's whole body or head three times, baptizes the candidate in the name of the Trinity."[104] In its execution, immersion would unfold as follows: the presider says "N., I baptize you in the name of the Father," as he immerses the candidate the first time, "and of the Son," as he immerses for a second time, "and of the Holy Spirit," as he immerses for a third time. If pouring is to be used, the following rubric is employed: "If baptism is by the pouring of water, either or both godparents place the right hand on the shoulder of the candidate, and the celebrant, taking baptismal water and pouring it three times on the candidate's bowed head, baptizes the candidate in the name of the Trinity."[105] An acclamation may be either sung or said by the assembly after each Baptism. Several of the acclamations from Sacred Scripture suggested by the rite are: "God is light: in him there is no darkness"; "God is love; those who live in love, live in God"; "Blessed be God who chose you in Christ"; and "You are God's work of art, created in Christ Jesus."[106]

Beyond the manner of Baptism, as well as the clear articulation of the baptismal formula for all in the church to hear, the presider must give consideration to the style by which he baptizes. Many will see the full immersion of a candidate under water as an aggressive

101. RCIA, 211.

102. RCIA, 224, 225.

103. RCIA, 225.

104. RCIA, 226.

105. RCIA, 226.

106. RCIA, 595.

action; certainly this outlook is perceived all the more when children or infants are thrust under water. While the symbolism of Baptism in water is that of dying to self in order to be reborn in Christ, it is important that the means of Baptism not appear to be violent. How the priest touches the elect and guides them into the water ought to convey the presence of Christ who comes to us gently and mercifully.

Immediately after arising from the waters, the newly baptized are in a very vulnerable state. Like newborns emerging from their mother's womb, those emerging from the font—often likened to a "womb" or a "tomb"—need immediate help in navigating their newfound place in the world. Thus, "the baptismal washing is followed by rites that give expression to the effects of the sacrament just received."[107] These "explanatory" rituals are meant to physically reveal to both those just baptized and the entire community the significance of what has taken place in the water. The first of these rituals is a postbaptismal anointing. This is done only if Confirmation is separated from Baptism. The only reason for such separation would be that the one who has been baptized has not reached catechetical age.[108] If this anointing takes place, it is to be done on the crown of the head, rather than on the forehead as in Confirmation.[109] A second explanatory rite is the clothing with a baptismal garment. After all the Baptisms have taken place, the godparents confer a white garment upon the newly baptized, while the presider states: "N. and N., you have become a new creation and have clothed yourselves in Christ. Receive this baptismal garment and bring it unstained to the judgment seat of our Lord Jesus Christ, so that you may have everlasting life."[110] Next is the presentation of a lighted candle that the godparent lights from the Easter candle. The priest addresses the newly baptized:

> You have been enlightened by Christ.
> Walk always as children of the light
> and keep the flame of faith alive in your hearts.
> When the Lord comes, may you go out to meet him
> with all the saints in the heavenly kingdom.[111]

---

107. RCIA, 214.
108. RCIA, 228.
109. RCIA, 228.
110. RCIA, 229.
111. RCIA, 230.

The connection of the sacraments is obvious as the minister of Baptism confers Confirmation.

The celebration of the sacraments of initiation continues with the celebration of Confirmation. One of the great treasures of the Easter Vigil is the inseparable link between Baptism and its sealing in Confirmation. Just as the Spirit descended upon Jesus at his baptism in the Jordan—(see Mark 1:9–10: "It happened in those days that Jesus came from Nazareth of Galilee and was baptized in the Jordan by John. On coming up out of the water he saw the heavens being torn open and the Spirit, like a dove, descending upon him.")—so does the Spirit fill the newly baptized with spiritual gifts. The RCIA states:

> In accord with the ancient practice followed in the Roman liturgy, adults are not to be baptized without receiving confirmation immediately afterward, unless some serious reason stands in the way. The conjunction of the two celebrations signifies the unity of the paschal mystery, the close link between the mission of the Son and the outpouring of the Holy Spirit, and the connection between the two sacraments through which the Son and the Holy Spirit come with the Father to those who are baptized.[112]

112. RCIA, 215.

This connection between Baptism and Confirmation is further exemplified in the regulation that the minister of Baptism is also to be the one who should confer Confirmation.[113]

The rite of Confirmation begins with an invitation spoken to the newly baptized, who have "become members of Christ and of his priestly people" and are now given the "promised strength of the Holy Spirit" in order to "be active members of the Church and to build up the Body of Christ in faith and love."[114] The presider turns to the assembly and asks them to pray that God the Father "will pour out the Holy Spirit on these newly baptized to strengthen them with his gifts and anoint them to be more like Christ, the Son of God."[115] After a period of silent prayer, the presider and all of the concelebrating priests stretch out their hands (called a "laying on of hands") over all those to be baptized, while the presider prays:

When the chrism flows abundantly at Confirmation, the confirmandi and the assembly are allowed to grasp the extravagance of God's love.

113. RCIA, 232.

114. RCIA, 233.

115. RCIA, 233.

Almighty God, Father of our Lord Jesus Christ,
who brought these your servants to new birth
by water and the Holy Spirit,
freeing them from sin:
send upon them, O Lord, the Holy Spirit, the Paraclete;
give them the spirit of wisdom and understanding,
the spirit of counsel and fortitude,
the spirit of knowledge and piety;
fill them with the spirit of the fear of the Lord.
Through Christ our Lord.

At the conclusion of this prayer, each candidate is anointed with chrism, as either or both godparents place the right hand on the shoulder of their respective candidate.[116] Anointing each neophyte with the cross on the forehead, the presider says: "N., be sealed with the Gift of the Holy Spirit." The newly confirmed responds, "Amen." The apostolic greeting follows with the presider adding, "Peace be with you," and the newly confirmed replying, "And with your Spirit." It is at this point that the neophytes, if baptized by immersion, depart from the assembly to put on their white garments.

Before continuing with the renewal of baptismal promises that follows the celebration of Confirmation, it might be helpful to add a few words on how the priest applies the chrism during Confirmation. The RCIA states: "The minister of the sacrament dips his right thumb in the chrism and makes the sign of the cross on the forehead of the one to be confirmed."[117] As with the suggestion that the elect ought to be baptized in an abundance of water, so the sealing of Baptism with the Spirit should convey the profusion of God's grace. In other words, the chrism should be used lavishly. The presider might consider the benefit of pouring the oil on the crown of the neophytes' heads and gently rubbing it upon their foreheads. Applying the chrism with a certain disregard for tidiness and efficiency not only allows the confirmandi to better feel the gift of the Spirit, it allows the Church to better see and smell God's unrestrained extravagance.

116. RCIA, 235.

117. RCIA, 235.

The next major component in the celebration of the sacraments of initiation is the renewal of baptismal promises. "After the celebration of Baptism (and Confirmation), the celebrant addresses the community, in order to invite those present to the renewal of their baptismal promises; the candidates for reception into full communion join the rest of the community in this renunciation of sin and profession of faith. All stand and hold lighted candles."[118] This is not an interruption of the celebration of the sacraments of initiation but rather is intrinsic to their execution; neophytes see that Baptism is renewed regularly in the assembly of the Church. The priest addresses the faithful in these or similar words:

> Dear brethren (brothers and sisters), through the Paschal Mystery
> we have been buried with Christ in Baptism,
> so that we may walk with him in newness of life.
> And so, now that our Lenten observance is concluded,
> let us renew the promises of Holy Baptism,
> by which we once renounced Satan and his works
> and promised to serve God in the holy catholic Church.[119]

The presider chooses between two formularies for the renunciation of sin, using the same interrogation that was used for the elect. The three questions of the first option found in *The Roman Missal* are: "Do you renounce Satan? And all his works? And all his empty show?" The questions for the second option are: "Do you renounce sin, so as to live in the freedom of the children of God? Do you renounce the lure of evil, so that sin may have no mastery over you? Do you renounce Satan, the author and prince of sin?" This leads immediately to the profession of faith, with the presider again asking a set of questions regarding belief.[120] The renewal concludes with the sprinkling of the people with the blessed water while they sing an appropriate song affirming its life-giving nature.[121] The priest ought to consider carefully how to "stir up" this gesture, making it as rich and full as possible. In many places, the entire assembly is invited to come to the baptismal font to wash themselves in the waters of new life.

---

118. RCIA, 237.
119. RM, Easter Vigil, 55.
120. RCIA, 239.
121. RCIA, 240.

Although neither the RCIA nor *The Roman Missal* suggest an entrance into the assembly of the faithful by the neophytes after they have donned their white garments, the time after the renewal of baptismal promises is most appropriate. *The Roman Missal* merely states: “Meanwhile the newly baptized are led to their place among the faithful.”[122] It would be most appropriate for the newly baptized to carry their lighted baptismal candles in a formal procession into the assembly, as the faithful joyfully welcome them with song. *The Roman Missal* states: “After the sprinkling, the Priest returns to the chair where, omitting the Creed, he directs the Universal Prayer, in which the newly baptized participate for the first time.”[123] This is no incidental moment in the lives of the neophytes; rather, they are assuming for the first time their baptismal responsibility to prayerfully make intercession on behalf of the Church and the entire world. They are full-fledged disciples.

The Liturgy of the Eucharist, which follows, serves as the full acceptance of the newly baptized to live in union with Christ and his Church. The RCIA offers the following theological summary of this ritual expression:

> Finally in the celebration of the eucharist, as they take part for the first time and with full right, the newly baptized reach the culminating point in their Christian initiation. In this eucharist the neophytes, now raised to the ranks of the royal priesthood, have an active part both in the general intercessions and, to the extent possible, in bringing the gifts to the altar. With the entire community they share in the offering of the sacrifice and say the Lord's Prayer, giving expression to the spirit of adoption as God's children that they have received in baptism. When in communion they receive the body that was given for us and the blood that was shed, the neophytes are strengthened in the gifts they have already received and are given a foretaste of the eternal banquet.[124]

For many of these men and women, who have been dismissed from the weekly assembly with words of joyful anticipation for “the day when you will share fully in the Lord's Table,” participation in the Liturgy of the Eucharist is experienced as a tremendous gift. The great joy seen upon the faces of the neophytes as they

122. RM, Easter Vigil, 57.

123. RM, Easter Vigil, 58.

124. RCIA, 217.

approach the altar as full members of Christ's Body serves as a reminder to the entire Church that the sustenance we receive on our pilgrim journey is never to be consumed without deep faith and hearts filled with thanksgiving. For this reason, special interpolations for Eucharistic Prayers I, II, and III (Eucharistic Prayer IV is not to be used during the Easter season) are given in *The Roman Missal* that help to give expression to the special significance of the Eucharist this night: Ritual Mass 1—For the Conferral of the Sacraments of Christian Initiation, Ritual Mass 3—For the Conferral of Baptism.[125] For the full symbolic act of participating in the Lord's sacrifice, "it is most desirable that the neophytes, together with their godparents, parents, spouses, and catechists, receive communion under both kinds."[126] Finally, the RCIA suggests that before the Lamb of God, the priest may "briefly remind the neophytes of the preeminence of the eucharist, which is the climax of their initiation and the center of the whole Christian life."[127]

125. RCIA, 242.

126. RCIA, 243.

127. RCIA, 243.

Chapter 6

Fourth Period: Mystagogy . . . and Life

The celebration of important passages in life, such as graduation, marriage, the birth of a child, or the death of a loved one entails a letting go of a former way of life to embrace a new outlook. As has been demonstrated in the structure of the *Rite of Christian Initiation of Adults*, this transition does not occur without the investment of time. Even at the end of the process, when one has reentered the world anew and has seen relationships reordered in Christ, time must be devoted to reflection and to the incorporation of the new way of life into one's being. "What did I experience throughout school that has made my diploma significant?" "What have I embraced in exchanging our wedding vows?" "How have the familydynamics shifted with the addition of a newborn?" "How can I truly grieve the death of the one I loved?" Although the celebration of crossing a significant threshold in life may signal change, embracing the consequences of that change takes the work of significant rumination.

This is precisely the nature of mystagogy. It is a time to ask the question: "What did I experience?" so that I might probe deeper into the mystery of Christian celebration and Christian life in general. Mystagogy is more than instruction on the liturgical rites—it is a stirring up of memory and imagination to make profound connections with personal life stories. The sixth chapter of the Apostle Paul's Letter to the Romans is mystagogical in nature:

> Are you unaware that we who were baptized into Christ Jesus were baptized into his death? We were indeed buried with him through baptism into death, so that, just as Christ was raised from the dead by the glory of the Father, we too might live in newness of life.[1]

The recipients of Paul's letter have already been baptized; they have lived through the sacramental experience. Furthermore, Paul uses rich imagery of burial and death to conjure an experience common to all: every person has an experience of the seriousness of death. Thus, without ever using the term "commitment," Paul calls the Romans to see that the "newness of life" given them requires a willingness to die to sin: "Therefore, sin must not reign over your mortal bodies so that you obey their desires."[2] Mystagogy uses evocative imagery to promote insight and discovery.

Period of Postbaptismal Catechesis or Mystagogy

The final period of time in the journey of conversion, as outlined by the *Rite of Christian Initiation of Adults*, is the period of postbaptismal catechesis or mystagogy. The newly baptized are now to be called "neophytes"; as newly born into the Christian faith and life in the Church, these are novices who continue to need nurturing and support. The period of mystagogy is also a time for the Church community as a whole to recognize that the Body of Christ has been transformed with the addition of new members. It is incumbent upon the parish priest to promote this mutual growth—the "new" and the "old" must recognize their resurrected life. Regarding the period of postbaptismal catechesis, the RCIA states:

> This is a time for the community and the neophytes together to grow in deepening their grasp of the paschal mystery and in making it part of their lives through meditation on the Gospel, sharing in the eucharist, and doing the works of charity. To strengthen the neophytes as they begin to walk in newness of life, the community of the faithful, their

1. Romans 6:3–4.
2. Romans 6:12.

> godparents, and their parish priests (pastors) should give them thoughtful and friendly help.[3]

The interconnection between the neophytes and the already baptized is a source of inspiration in the days of Easter joy, when the Church realizes itself anew. This inspiration is expressed in paragraph 246:

> Just as their new participation in the sacraments enlightens the neophytes' understanding of the Scriptures, so too it increases their contact with the rest of the faithful and has an impact on the experience of the community. As a result, interaction between the neophytes and the faithful is made easier and more beneficial. The period of postbaptismal catechesis is of great significance for both the neophytes and the rest of the faithful. Through it the neophytes, with the help of their godparents, should experience a full and joyful welcome into the community and enter into closer ties with the other faithful. The faithful, in turn, should derive from it a renewal of inspiration and of outlook.[4]

The Christian initiation process is considered by many to be the means by which a parish experiences ongoing renewal. The chief practices listed earlier—meditation on the Gospel, sharing in the Eucharist, and doing works of charity—are basic disciplines that pertain to each member of Christ. Because focused attention must be paid to assisting the neophytes in making these practices the pattern of their lives, the Church as a whole is inspired to reinvigorate herself according to the Gospel, the Eucharist, and self-sacrificial service.

As suggested earlier, the word "mystagogy" conveys the sense of "mystery" and is understood to be a reflection on what one has experienced. The preaching of the great mystagogues—Cyril of Jerusalem, John Chrysostom, Theodore of Mopsuestia, Ambrose, and Augustine—reveals a zealous concern for helping the newly baptized probe the depths of what they experienced in the waters of the font and around the table of plenty. For example, Ambrose preaches to the neophytes regarding their experience of the Eucharist:

> What happened after this? You can approach the altar. When you have arrived, you can see what you could not see before. This is the mystery of

3. RCIA, 244.

4. RCIA, 246.

which you have read in the gospel . . . Now you too must think about your eyes; the eyes of your heart. With your bodily eye you saw bodily things, but you were not yet able to see sacramental things with the eyes of your heart. . . You went there, you washed, you came to the altar, you began to see what you had not seen before: that is to say, through the font of the Lord and the preaching of the Lord's passion, at that moment your eyes were opened. Before, you seemed to be blind of heart; but now you began to perceive the light of the sacraments.[5]

Mystagogical preaching helps people to see with the eyes of the heart.

Thus, it could be said that "mystagogy" is the celebration of a new way of seeing, a way of seeing with the eyes of the heart. The mystagogues treated the neophytes with great care and wanted to help them discover the grandeur of the new world they entered when they ascended from the waters of the font. The period of postbaptismal catechesis or mystagogy ought to be no less demanding in the twenty-first century. Preaching throughout the entire Easter season ought to take the form of mystagogical preaching, helping all to see with the eyes of the heart.

Thus, pastors are to ensure that the newly baptized are given plenty of opportunity to share their experience of the Easter Vigil and are guided to draw connections to the Word of God. The the ritual text suggests that lived experience is of greater value than accumulated information:

The neophytes are, as the term "mystagogy" suggests, introduced into a fuller and more effective understanding of mysteries through the Gospel message they have learned and above all through their experience of the sacraments they have received. For they have truly been renewed in

5. Yarnold, *The Awe-Inspiring Rites of Initiation*, 125–127.

> mind, tasted more deeply the sweetness of God's word, received the fellowship of the Holy Spirit, and grown to know the goodness of the Lord. Out of this experience, which belongs to Christians and increases as it is lived, they derive a new perception of the faith, of the Church, and of the world.[6]

Again, the process of mystagogy offers the opportunity for ecclesial renewal. Imagine what our Sunday mornings would look like if every celebration of the Eucharist was followed by a time of mystagogy, in which people were encouraged to share what they heard, saw, and felt within the liturgy. Such reflection would help members of Christ's Body to extend the liturgy into their daily lives, to experience the words of the Gospel as their story, and to desire to come together regularly for refreshment and renewal. Imagine the assistance that would be given to the priest for the preparation of his Sunday homilies if he had deeper insight into the mysterious ways in which people experience the movement of the Spirit.

However, priests are generally exhausted after the celebration of the Triduum. The expectation to move into a period of reflection on what has taken place in the spiritual lives of the neophytes is often a difficult one to fulfill. Keeping the joy of the Resurrection on the forefront of the minds of Christians for the fifty days of the Easter season is nearly impossible in a culture ready to move on to the next thing. Yet this is the responsibility of the pastor, to ensure that a suitable period of postbaptismal catechesis is provided for those new to the faith. The pastor is charged with maintaining the "distinctive spirit" of paschal joy in the entire community:

> Since the distinctive spirit and power of the period of postbaptismal catechesis or mystagogy derive from the new, personal experience of the sacraments and of the community, its main setting is the so-called Masses for neophytes, that is, the Sunday Masses of the Easter season. Besides being occasions for the newly baptized to gather with the community and share in the mysteries, these celebrations include particularly suitable readings from the Lectionary, especially the readings for Year A. Even when Christian initiation has been celebrated outside the usual times, the texts for these Sunday Masses of the Easter season may be used.[7]

---

6. RCIA, 245.
7. RCIA, 247.

For the neophytes, who have been accustomed to being dismissed to pray and reflect upon the Word of God apart from the Eucharistic assembly, there may be a certain longing for the intimacy of this small group. They had shared significant life stories with one another, no doubt experienced moments of vulnerability, and had come to discover a growing relationship with Christ in their common discernment. Now they are to navigate their way through the entire Mass without this gathering. The pastor needs to reflect on how to guarantee that the neophytes do not simply fall through the cracks in the aftermath of Holy Week and Easter.

Taking the work of mystagogy seriously and deliberately carving out the time for postbaptismal gatherings helps the parish extend the joy of Easter beyond Easter Sunday. Mystagogy helps mark the fifty days of Easter as a time of new discovery for the Church. The pastor should, therefore, designate particular Masses within the Easter season as Masses designed for the neophytes. The RCIA states:

> All the neophytes and their godparents should make an effort to take part in the Masses for the neophytes and the entire local community should be invited to participate with them. Special places in the congregation are to be reserved for the neophytes and their godparents. The homily and, as circumstances suggest, the general intercessions should take into account the presence and needs of the neophytes.[8]

The simple suggestion of designing the intercessions of the Universal Prayer with the presence of the neophytes in mind hints at the care the newly baptized deserve. Once again, it is not uncommon for neophytes to fall through the cracks in the days and weeks following the Vigil. Encouraging their presence at the Sunday celebration of the Eucharist and providing designated places within the assembly for them is the approach of a pastor who is attentive to his flock and does not want even one of his lambs to wander astray.

The *Rite of Christian Initiation of Adults* provides for other opportunities to "stir up the waters" for the neophytes after the conclusion of the period of postbaptismal catechesis (that is, the fifty days of the Easter season). For instance, the rite suggests that "to close the period of postbaptismal catechesis, some sort of

8. RCIA, 248.

celebration should be held at the end of the Easter season near Pentecost Sunday; festivities in keeping with local custom may accompany the occasion."[9] In addition to a celebration that accompanies their initial reception of the Easter sacraments, the parish ought to provide for fellowship toward the conclusion of the Easter season that celebrates the blossoming life of the neophytes. Mystagogy is about experience, and the experience of Christian fellowship is an important aspect of their ongoing journey into Christian life.

The RCIA mandates that the first anniversary of the neophytes' Baptism should be celebrated: "On the anniversary of their baptism the neophytes should be brought together in order to give thanks to God, to share with one another their spiritual experiences, and to renew their commitment."[10] Similarly, the bishop is asked to celebrate the Eucharist with the neophytes within a year after their Baptism: "To show his pastoral concern for these new members of the Church, the bishop, particularly if he was unable to preside at the sacraments of initiation himself, should arrange, if possible, to meet the recently baptized at least once in the year and to preside at a celebration of the eucharist with them."[11] Both of these suggestions illumine the vulnerability of those newly grafted onto Christ; for at least a year, they are to be nurtured with deliberate care.

Therefore, it is most appropriate that pastors schedule time within this year to meet with each of the neophytes individually to counsel them and to offer them ongoing support. Too often, men and women who are still wet from the font are tapped for various ministries in the parish. They might be asked to fulfill such liturgical roles as reader or extraordinary minister of the Eucharist, or they might be requested to join the finance council or a peace and social justice commission. Often, they are thrust into these ministries too early, before they have grown accustomed to their new way of life. Thus, the pastor helps to discern whether neophytes are truly ready for service or perhaps need more growth before taking on public responsibilities. Marriages can also change after one member has discovered a new relationship with Christ and the Church; pastors

9. RCIA, 249.

10. RCIA, 250.

11. RCIA, 251.

ought to be ready to assist in helping neophytes navigate potentially rocky waters. The bottom line is that priests must consider how they might best reach out to offer their full encouragement to all those who are new to the faith.

Mystagogy as a Rule for Life

The experience of mystagogy, as outlined by the RCIA, reveals the great hope for ongoing sacramental/liturgical renewal of the Church. All sacraments celebrate a life transition and thus may be seen as forms of ritual passage. However, a problem with our sacramental experience is that many times sacraments are considered something to be received rather than something to be lived. Once received, they are often forgotten, and thus ongoing immersion into the life of Christ does not follow. However, the Christian initiation process demonstrates that the sacraments of initiation are not simply imparted at the Easter Vigil, rather they begin to unfold then. As pastors experience the fruits of mystagogy, through their imaginative preaching and through hearing the experience of the neophytes, they see that the life of the Church is best organized when it is able to reflect as a community upon the intersection between sacramental experience and daily life.

In *Saying Amen: A Mystagogy of Sacrament*, Kathleen Hughes suggests that mystagogy is an ancient method that needs to be restored in our celebration of all the liturgies of the Church. She identifies several characteristics of mystagogy that are worthy for reflection. First, she contends, as has already been suggested and is articulated in the RCIA, that mystagogy is for all the baptized.[12] Hughes writes: "[C]ommunal reflection such as this is a healthy antidote to a privatized religion and a tendency on the part of North Americans to rugged individualism, especially when it comes to communicating deeply held religious insights and convictions."[13] Pastors who are able to engage the parish in a process of communal reflection will help make the Paschal Mystery come alive in church and at home. This is a primary benefit of the mystagogical method.

12. Kathleen Hughes, *Saying Amen: A Mystagogy of Sacrament* (Chicago: Liturgy Training Publications, 1999), 13.

13. Ibid, 13.

Just as the Eucharist is the endpoint of the adult experience of initiation, and its weekly (and/or daily) celebration demonstrates that initiation into Christ is never complete, so too does mystagogy demonstrate that catechesis does not end at the font or after Confirmation. Thus, a second characteristic of mystagogy is that learning never ends. The *National Statutes for the Catechumenate* underscores this in terms of the outreach given to the neophytes after the period of formal postbaptismal catechesis: "After the immediate mystagogy or postbaptismal catechesis during the Easter season, the program for the neophytes should extend until the anniversary of Christian initiation, with at least monthly assemblies of the neophytes for their deeper Christian formation and incorporation into the full life of the Christian community."[14] Do members of the Body of Christ, who have been celebrating the Eucharist for years, truly understand the nature and meaning of what they are doing in their singing, gesturing, and praying? Learning as a lifelong process demands that opportunities for catechesis be provided for all the faithful.

Liturgical participation holds open a sacramental way of living.

14. NS, 24.

A third characteristic of mystagogy as a way of life is that liturgical participation holds open a sacramental way of living. In other words, the more one discovers how to celebrate the Paschal Mystery—the Suffering, Death, and Resurrection of Christ—in the liturgy, the more one understands how to live the Paschal Mystery daily. As stated earlier, the RCIA envisions the following effect upon neophytes as a result of their liturgical participation: they have been "renewed in mind, tasted more deeply the sweetness of God's word, received the fellowship of the Holy Spirit, and grown to know the goodness of the Lord."[15] Hughes writes: "All of this spirit and power derives from the personal experience of the sacraments, which only increases as it is lived, opening participants to an ever-deeper understanding of the death and rising of Jesus Christ, the community of believers, the faith we cherish and the world we long to transform in God's name."[16] "Full, conscious, and active" participation in the liturgy, as called for in paragraph 14 of the *Constitution on the Sacred Liturgy*, and mystagogy go hand in hand when there is the desire to peer deeper into the mysteries.

Another characteristic of a mystagogical method for sacramental celebration, one which has already been alluded to, is that all seven sacraments need to include a time of reflection after they have been experienced. As an example, we can consider the Sacrament of Matrimony. While much time may be spent preparing a couple for the wedding liturgy, including counseling with a priest, time spent with married couples, a retreat, and so forth, little investment of time is given to the couple after they exchange their vows. Hughes writes: "Surely every sacrament invites us to deepen our own conversion and to commit ourselves anew to a vision of God's reign."[17] Imagine how the Church might recommit herself to the beauty of married life if she could hear the story of those who had recently celebrated the Sacrament of Matrimony. Imagine how the newly married couple could begin to understand their marriage as a vocation if they could share their experience. The Christian initiation process challenges us to think about the nature of sacraments

15. RCIA, 245.

16. Hughes, 14.

17. Hughes, 14.

in a renewed light—they are to bond the Body of Christ ever closer as one for the outward healing of this world's brokenness and pain.

A fifth characteristic that Hughes discusses is that personal experience is conveyed in symbol, in a language that is "more like poetry than prose."[18] For this very reason, the liturgy is filled with symbols and imagery. When it comes to expressing meaningful experiences in our lives, we resort to metaphors for expression. In turn, employing symbolic language allows others to connect with the experience at various levels; metaphor helps to enflesh personal experience. Hughes writes:

> The key to mystagogical reflection is that it is subjective rather than objective; it is about my experience and your experience of an encounter with God through the sacramental celebration. The mystagogical task is to enable the newly baptized to reflect on their personal experience of celebration and what it triggered in their inner world, to move from a vague awareness of the mystery dimension of their lives to a greater conceptual and affective clarity, and to find a proper way to continue to allow experience and expression to inform one another. Only through a pooling of our experiences will we have anything even approaching a full sense of the presence and power of God active in those who believe.[19]

No two people experience the liturgy the same way, and no two people walk the same path on the journey of life. For example, the full immersion of a baby may be seen by some people in the assembly as a beautiful moment of birth, while others may see the action as violent and aggressive. If we do not talk about the multivalent nature of symbols, but only about objective truth, we turn God into an idol rather than a mystery to be adored.

Finally, each of these characteristics hinges upon a remaining characteristic that is critical for the project of ongoing ecclesial renewal, and is particularly valuable for pastors: mystagogy demands that the sacraments and all the rites of the Church be celebrated well. "Good liturgy," writes Hughes, "is an absolute prerequisite to rich symbolic participation and contemplation."[20] It is hard to be attentive at a level that is contemplative if our assemblies are not fully engaged in singing, if preaching is poorly prepared

18. Hughes, 15.
19. Hughes, 15.
20. Hughes, 16.

or is inflammatory, and if symbols are withered and decayed. Good liturgy will move the imagination to probe deeper. The *General Instruction of the Roman Missal* clearly states:

> Since, however, the celebration of the Eucharist, like the entire Liturgy, is carried out by means of perceptible signs by which the faith is nourished, strengthened, and expressed, the greatest care is to be taken that those forms and elements proposed by the Church are chosen and arranged, which, given the circumstances of persons and places, more effectively foster active and full participation and more aptly respond to the spiritual needs of the faithful.[21]

Much the same is said later in the General Instruction regarding the distribution of duties for the preparation of liturgical celebrations:

> There should be harmony and diligence among all those involved in the effective preparation of each liturgical celebration in accordance with the Missal and other liturgical books, both as regards the rites and as regards the pastoral and musical aspects. This should take place under the direction of the rector of the church and after consultation with the faithful in the things that directly pertain to them.[22]

Therefore, the pastor has the responsibility to maintain a high quality of liturgical celebration within the parish, a quality based on allowing each member of Christ's Body to offer his or her gifts for the good of the community. Providing for rich symbolism and life-giving rites does not mean organizing performances that allow people to sit back and watch as spectators; rather, ongoing liturgical renewal calls for a liturgy that spirals people into mystery, as the presence of Christ is contemplated in word and action, sight and sound, touch and smell. Thus, each act of liturgical celebration calls for presiders who are fundamentally aware of all that is taking place and are humble enough to bow to the Spirit alone, who makes Christ known.

Hughes suggests that, in the end, mystagogy as a rule of life is all about "paying attention." It is about seeing all of life through the eyes of the heart, attempting to make sense of the ordinariness of daily living through the extra-ordinariness of the Suffering, Death, and Resurrection of Christ. This is the passage that all sacraments celebrate: our lives being refashioned according to a willingness to

21. *General Instruction of the Roman Missal* (GIRM), 20.

22. GIRM, 111.

die to self in order to be raised to new life in Christ. Hughes writes: "Liturgical attention is of two kinds: attending to the liturgy as it unfolds and attending to the movements of our hearts before, during and after the celebration."[23] Mystagogy—that is "paying attention"—links liturgy to life. Our learning, our initiation, is never complete until we have come to that final discovery which is the banquet feast of heaven.

23. Hughes, 17.

Chapter 7

Other Pastoral Considerations: Christians Seeking Full Communion, Children of Catechetical Age, and Marriage Issues

This final chapter is devoted to a cursory exploration of the material found in Part II of the *Rite of Christian Initiation of Adults*, "Rites for Particular Circumstances." The contents here are designed to help priests maintain a certain pastoral sensitivity that respects those seeking to embrace the Catholic way of life but who cannot simply be folded into the process of journeying with the unbaptized on the way to the font. Pastoral sensitivity also needs to guide a pastor's heart when dealing with situations surrounding marriage that need attention prior to the celebration of the sacraments of initiation. All in all, this final section calls pastors to be filled with an ingenuity that is respectful of tradition in attempting to tailor Christian formation to individual needs.

An example of the RCIA's promotion of a spirit of ingenuity is found in the chapter "Christian Initiation of Adults in Exceptional Circumstances."[1] Although mentioned earlier, this section suggests that "extraordinary circumstances," such as "sickness, old age, change of residence, long absence for travel" may be reasons for a bishop to grant permission to an "expanded form" of initiation.[2] This expansion "makes it possible for a candidate who had begun the catechumenate with others, but was forced to interrupt it, to complete the catechumenate alone by celebrating, in addition to the sacraments of initiation, elements from the full rite."[3] Nevertheless, even when this accommodation is made, the rite instructs that there be no shortchange of catechesis, that the rites be celebrated publicly, and that postbaptismal catechesis take place.[4] Likewise, this section also permits an "abbreviated form" of the rite: "This rite includes elements that express the presentation and welcoming of the candidate and that also express the candidate's clear and firm resolve to request Christian initiation, as well as the Church's approval of the candidate."[5] An abbreviated rite would be celebrated only in the situation in which someone is known to "have gone through an adequate period of instruction and preparation before baptism"[6] in another community. As in the expanded form, the abbreviated form is not to be used as a shortcut but is to be used in those exceptional situations caused by a change in community or a period away from the community.

Another exceptional circumstance treated by the rite and given its own section is when a person is in danger of death. "Persons, whether catechumens or not, who are in danger of death but are not at the point of death and so are able to hear and answer the questions involved may be baptized with this short rite."[7] Once again, this situation of pastoral sensitivity is not to be employed to give people a shortcut, as "they must also promise that upon

1. RCIA, 331–339.
2. RCIA, 332.
3. RCIA, 333.
4. RCIA, 335.
5. RCIA, 337.
6. RCIA, 336.
7. RCIA, 370.

recovery they will go through the complete program of initiation as it applies to them."[8] In situations of extreme emergency, the priest should administer all three sacraments of initiation (if chrism is at hand and the Eucharist is available).[9] "In the case of a person who is at the point of death, that is, whose death is imminent, and time is short, the minister, omitting everything else, pours natural water (even if not blessed) on the head of the sick person, while saying the usual sacramental form."[10]

The situations noted here are clearly atypical for celebrating adult initiation. However, they make clear that a pastor must make decisions regarding what constitutes readiness on the part of candidates for Baptism and when life crises call for outreach that supersedes the following of timelines and rules. Far more challenging, however, is the question of how to fold baptized, yet uncatechized adults, either Catholic or from other Christian communities, into the initiation mission of the parish.

Christians Seeking Full Communion

One of the biggest mistakes those responsible for adult formation make is lumping together adults who already have been baptized with catechumens. For example, someone baptized as a Methodist shows interest in joining the Catholic Church. It might seem logical and efficient to have this person join a group of seekers who are in the initial stage of asking questions regarding Christ and faith. The problem is that the Methodist has already been baptized and, therefore, has an established relationship with Jesus Christ. The dignity of Baptism demands that the person's previous background be respected. The same holds true for a Catholic who was baptized as an infant but never received catechesis. That Catholic must not simply be placed in the catechumenate. The RCIA states:

> Even though uncatechized adults have not yet heard the message of the mystery of Christ, their status differs from that of catechumens, since by baptism they have already become members of the Church and children

8. RCIA, 371.
9. RCIA, 372.
10. RCIA, 373.

> of God. Hence their conversion is based on the baptism they have already received, the effects of which they must develop.[11]

Pastors must work to ensure that the process of catechesis for a baptized candidate for full communion is clearly differentiated from the catechumenate. The *National Statutes for the Catechumenate* further underscores the importance of distinguishing already baptized Christians from catechumens:

> Those who have already been baptized in another Church or ecclesial community should not be treated as catechumens or so designated. Their doctrinal and spiritual preparation for reception into full Catholic communion should be determined according to the individual case, that is, it should depend on the extent to which the baptized person has led a Christian life within a community of faith and has been appropriately catechized to deepen his or her inner adherence to the Church.[12]

Nevertheless, the Church owes baptized yet uncatechized adults a suitable process of formation; they are not to be rushed to the Sacraments of Confirmation and Communion. The RCIA clearly states:

> As in the case of catechumens, the preparation of these adults requires a considerable time, during which the faith infused in baptism must grow in them and take deep root through the pastoral formation they receive. A program of training, catechesis suited to their needs, contact with the community of the faithful, and participation in certain liturgical rites are needed in order to strengthen them in the Christian faith.[13]

The key here is to determine what kind of catechesis and training is best "suited to their needs." For example, while baptized yet uncatechized adults may be dismissed from the liturgical assembly in order to "participate in celebrations of the word together with catechumens,"[14] they must not be confused with catechumens. Even though they have not yet received from the Lord's Table, they still have the right to be present for the Liturgy of the Eucharist. When and how, therefore, should catechesis and training take place?

---

11. RCIA, 400.
12. NS, 30.
13. RCIA, 401.
14. NS, 31.

The rite answers this question: "For the most part the plan of catechesis corresponds to the one laid down for the catechumens. But in the process of catechesis the priest, deacon, or catechist should take into account that these adults have a special status because they are already baptized."[15] *The National Statutes for the Catechumenate* offers the following recommendation:

> Those who have been baptized but have received relatively little Christian upbringing may participate in the elements of catechumenal formation so far as necessary and appropriate, but should not take part in rites intended for the unbaptized catechumens. . . . Those baptized persons who have lived as Christians and need only instruction in the Catholic tradition and a degree of probation within the Catholic community should not be asked to undergo a full program parallel to the catechumenate.[16]

Individuals may be ready at various times of the year to be received into the full communion of the Catholic Church.

The uniqueness of each individual situation demands that pastors connect with the already baptized yet uncatechized in discussions of mutual discernment. It would be most helpful for pastors to inquire regularly from these individuals what they need from the Church to

15. RCIA, 402.
16. NS, 31.

reach a point in their faith in which they are ready for full communion. This means that individuals will be ready for full communion at various times throughout the year; thus, the rite for receiving them fully into the Church might best be celebrated apart from the Easter Vigil. This expectation is clearly outlined in the *National Statutes:*

> It is preferable that reception into full communion not take place at the Easter Vigil lest there be any confusion of such baptized Christians with the candidates for baptism, possible misunderstandings of or even reflection upon the sacrament of baptism celebrated in another Church or ecclesial community, or any perceived triumphalism in the liturgical welcome into the Catholic eucharistic community.[17]

The primary way in which the RCIA distinguishes those preparing for Baptism and those preparing for full communion is through the rites celebrated in the liturgical assembly. Thus, four celebrations are developed in the RCIA that are meant to be part of the formation of the uncatechized but already baptized: (1) Rite of Welcoming, (2) Rite of Calling the Candidates to Continuing Conversion, (3) Penitential Rite, and (4) Reception of Baptized Christians into the Full Communion of the Catholic Church. Familiarity with these rites will help pastors to uphold the status of the already baptized and will help to ignite ways in which the already baptized can be catechized through a process that "corresponds to the one laid down for catechumens"[18] but is unique unto itself.

Just as the Church wishes to mark the successful completion of a time of inquiry for those seeking faith, it also seeks to provide a public welcome for those already baptized adults who desire the sacraments of Confirmation and Eucharist or who wish to be received into the full communion of the Catholic Church. The foundation of this gesture of welcome and hospitality is the acknowledgment that those to be welcomed are already a part of the community "because they have already been marked with the seal of baptism."[19] The RCIA continues to underscore this dimension of the Church's welcome:

17. NS, 33.
18. RCIA, 402.
19. RCIA, 405.

> The prayers and ritual gestures acknowledge that such candidates are already part of the community because they have been marked by baptism. Now the Church surrounds them with special care and support as they prepare to be sealed with the gift of the Spirit in confirmation and take their place at the banquet table of Christ's sacrifice.[20]

While the *Rite of Christian Initiation of Adults* provides a combined Rite of Welcome with the Rite of Acceptance into the Order of Catechumens (Appendix I), employing this option blurs the distinction between Christians and the unbaptized. Thus, celebrating a separate rite of welcoming at various times throughout the year seems to be most pastorally appropriate.

The structure of the Rite of Welcoming the Candidates is as follows:

Welcoming the Candidates

- Greeting
- Opening Dialogue
- Candidates' Declaration of Intent
- Affirmation by the Sponsors and the Assembly
- Signing of the Candidates with the Cross
    - Signing of the Forehead
    - Signing of the Other Senses (optional)
    - Concluding Prayer

Liturgy of the Word

- Instruction
- Readings
- Homily
- Presentation of a Bible (optional)
- Profession of Faith
- General Intercessions
- Prayer over the Candidates
- Dismissal of the Assembly (when the rite takes place within a celebration of the Word)

Liturgy of the Eucharist

20. RCIA, 412.

Rather than examining each ritual component of this celebration, which has distinct parallels to the structure of the Rite of Acceptance, it is sufficient to highlight the way in which the Rite of Welcoming underscores the dignity of those already baptized into Christ.

First of all, taking place within the context of the Sunday assembly (although it may also be celebrated within the Celebration of the Word of God), the location of the Rite of Welcoming is noticeably different from that of the Rite of Acceptance. The RCIA states: "Because they are already numbered among the baptized, the candidates are seated in a prominent place among the faithful."[21] This rite does not begin at the threshold of the church because these individuals have already been attached to Christ. Furthermore, the rubrics suggest that the presider, in welcoming the candidates with "joy and happiness," is to remind the assembly "that these candidates have already been baptized."[22] The presider ought to carefully consider how his words of welcome might honor the Christian traditions from which the candidates have come. "If it seems opportune, he may also indicate briefly the particular path that has led the candidates to seek the completion of their Christian initiation."[23]

After an opening dialogue in which the presider asks the candidates to state their names and what they ask of the Church, he either asks them to declare, in their own words, the reasons why they are seeking full participation in the life of the Church or to respond affirmatively to the following declaration of intent:

> Blessed be the God and Father of our Lord Jesus Christ, who, in his great mercy has given us a new birth unto a living hope, a hope which draws its life from Christ's resurrection from the dead. By baptism into Christ Jesus, this hope of glory became your own. Christ opened for you the way of the Gospel that leads to eternal life. Now, under the guidance of the Holy Spirit, you desire to continue that journey of faith.
>
> Are you prepared to reflect more deeply on the mystery of your baptism, to listen with us to the apostles' instruction, and to join with us in a life of prayer and service?[24]

21. RCIA, 416.
22. RCIA, 417.
23. RCIA, 417.
24. RCIA, 419, Option A.

Notice within this declaration of intent the dignity accorded the Baptism by which the candidates have lived up to this point: "this hope of glory became your own," "Christ opened for you the way of the Gospel," "you desire to continue that journey of faith." The words of the Church honor what has previously constituted the life of the already baptized and locates it within the context of an ongoing journey.

The sponsors and the assembly affirm the decision of the candidates to progress toward full communion in the Church, which is concluded by a prayer of thanksgiving on the part of the presider. Next, the candidates are signed with the cross on their foreheads. However, there is no sense that they are receiving the cross for the first time; rather, they receive the cross as a reminder of their Baptism: "Receive the cross on your forehead as a reminder of your baptism into Christ's saving death and resurrection."[25] At the end of the signing, the priest concludes either with the opening prayer for the Mass of the day or the following prayer:

> Almighty God,
> by the cross and resurrection of your Son
> you have given life to your people.
>
> In baptism these your servants accepted
> the sign of the cross:
> make them living proof of its saving power
> and help them to persevere in the footsteps of Christ.
>
> We ask this through Christ our Lord.[26]

The Liturgy of the Word proceeds as usual after the presider "speaks briefly to the candidates and their sponsors, helping them to understand the dignity of God's word proclaimed and heard in the church."[27] The Liturgy of the Word concludes with general intercessions that include one or more intentions for the candidates. The intercessions conclude with a prayer that acknowledges the candidates as belonging to a family of faith. The priest utters the prayer with his hands extended over the candidates:

25. RCIA, 422.

26. RCIA, 424.

27. RCIA, 425.

> Almighty and eternal God,
> whose love gathers us together as one,
> receive the prayers of your people.
>
> Look kindly on these your servants,
> already consecrated to you in baptism,
> and draw them into the fullness of faith.
>
> Keep your family one in the bonds of love
> through Christ our Lord.[28]

The Liturgy of the Eucharist proceeds as usual. If the Rite of Welcoming takes place within the celebration of the Word of God, the entire assembly is dismissed at this time.

A second rite that is meant to be celebrated with the already baptized, and that publicly acknowledges the dignity of their Baptism, is the Rite of Sending the Candidates for Recognition by the Bishop and the Call to Continuing Conversion. To demonstrate unity within the process of initiation, those seeking to complete initiation in the celebration of the Easter sacraments are sent by the local parish to be recognized and affirmed by the local bishop:

> Because he is the sign of unity within the particular Church, it is fitting for the bishop to recognize these candidates. It is the responsibility of the parish community, however, to prepare the candidates for their fuller life in the Church. Through the experience of worship, daily life, and service in the parish community the candidates deepen their appreciation of the Church's tradition and universal character.[29]

The Rite of Sending "offers that local community the opportunity to express its joy in the candidates' decision and to send them forth to the celebration of recognition assured of the parish's care and support."[30] Although the Rite of Sending candidates for recognition may be combined with the Rite of Sending Catechumens for Election (Appendix I, 2), it is most appropriate to celebrate it as a separate liturgy.

---

28. RCIA, 431.
29. RCIA, 435.
30. RCIA, 435.

The structure for the Rite of Sending the Candidates for Recognition by the Bishop and for the Call to Continuing Conversion is as follows:

Liturgy of the Word

- Homily
- Presentation of the Candidates
- Affirmation by the Sponsors [and the Assembly (optional)]
- General intercessions
- Prayer over the Candidates
- Dismissal of the Assembly (optional)

Liturgy of the Eucharist

The homily "should be suited to the actual situation and should address not just the candidates but the entire community of the faithful, so that all will be encouraged to give good example and to accompany the candidates along the path leading to their complete initiation."[31] After the homily, the person most directly responsible for the formation of the candidates presents them to the presider and to the community as a whole. The presider then invites the candidates forward with their sponsors and addresses the assembly and, in particular, the sponsors in these or similar words:

> My dear friends, these candidates, already one with us by reason of their baptism in Christ, have asked to complete their initiation (or: to be received into the full communion of the Catholic Church). Those who know them have judged them to be sincere in their desire. During the period of their catechetical formation they have listened to the word of Christ and endeavored to follow his commands more perfectly; they have shared the company of the Christian brothers and sisters in this community and joined with them in prayer.
>
> And so I announce to all of you here that our community ratifies their desire to complete their initiation (or: to be received into full communion).[32]

The presider seeks the affirmation of the candidates by their sponsors, calls on the entire assembly to express its approval of the

31. RCIA, 438.
32. RCIA, 440.

candidates through applause or some other gesture, and then concludes by announcing to the candidates that they are now to be sent to the bishop who will invite them "to live in deeper conformity to the life of Christ."[33] The general intercessions that follow conclude with the following prayer over the candidates:

> Father of love and power,
> it is your will to establish everything in Christ
> and to draw us into his all-embracing love.
>
> Guide these candidates in the days and weeks ahead:
> strengthen them in their vocation,
> build them into the kingdom of your Son,
> and seal them with the Spirit of your promise.
>
> We ask this through Christ our Lord.[34]

The Liturgy of the Eucharist proceeds as usual. This Rite of Sending is meant as a prelude to the celebration of the recognition by the bishop and for his call to continuing conversion. However, it is possible for parishes to celebrate the Rite of Calling the Candidates to Continuing Conversion, especially in parishes in which there are no catechumens.[35] This rite is to be celebrated if the decision is made not to send the candidates to the bishop for recognition.

The structure of the Rite of Calling the Candidates to Continuing Conversion is as follows:

Liturgy of the Word

- Homily
- Presentation of the Candidates for Confirmation and Eucharist
- Affirmation by the Sponsors [and the Assembly (optional)]
- Act of Recognition
- General Intercessions
- Prayer over the Candidates
- Dismissal of the Assembly (when this occurs at a Liturgy of the Word)

Liturgy of the Eucharist

33. RCIA, 441.
34. RCIA, 443.
35. RCIA, 447.

To be celebrated at the beginning of Lent, with the pastor as the presider, the Rite of Calling the Candidates to Continuing Conversion celebrates the recognition of the candidates as being ready to "participate fully in the sacramental life of the Catholic Church."[36] Structured very similarly to the rite of sending to the bishop, the Rite of Calling the Candidates to Continuing Conversion includes this verbal act of recognition, in which the pastor addresses both candidates and sponsors:

> N. and N., the Church recognizes your desire (to be sealed with the gift of the Holy Spirit and) to have a place at Christ's eucharistic table. Join with us this Lent in a spirit of repentance. Hear the Lord's call to conversion and be faithful to your baptismal covenant.
>
> Sponsors, continue to support these candidates with your guidance and concern. May they see in you a love for the Church and a sincere desire for doing good. Lead them this Lent to the joys of the Easter mysteries.[37]

After the praying of the general intercessions, in which one or more prayers are added for the candidates in particular, a prayer over the candidates concludes the rite and leads into the Liturgy of the Eucharist. The prayer suggests the ongoing "conformity" to the life of Christ:

> Lord God,
> whose love brings us to life
> and whose mercy gives us new birth,
> look favorably upon these candidates,
> and conform their lives
> to the pattern of Christ's suffering.
> May he become their wealth and wisdom,
> and may they know in their lives
> the power flowing from his resurrection,
> who is Lord for ever and ever.[38]

A parochial celebration of the Rite of Calling the Candidates to Continuing Conversion not only affirms the dignity of the individual's Baptism, it also encourages the entire parish to see itself called to continuing conversion. All Christians are called to "conform their

36. RCIA, 452.
37. RCIA, 454.
38. RCIA, 456.

lives to the pattern of Christ's suffering," and all Christians recognize this as a daily invitation.

Another ritual celebration intended for baptized but previously uncatechized adults is a Penitential Rite (Scrutiny). Similar to the scrutinies for catechumens, the penitential rite is to be celebrated either in a Mass or in a celebration of the Word of God.[39] Designed to be celebrated on the Second Sunday of Lent, it also may take place on a Lenten weekday.[40] The RCIA states:

> This penitential rite is intended solely for celebrations with baptized adults preparing for confirmation and eucharist or reception into the full communion of the Catholic Church. Because the prayer of exorcism in the three scrutinies for catechumens who have received the Church's election properly belongs to the elect and uses numerous images referring to their approaching baptism, those scrutinies of the elect and this penitential rite for those preparing for confirmation and eucharist have been kept separate and distinct.[41]

Thus, while the scrutinies are meant to prepare the elect for Baptism, the penitential rite has the purpose of preparing the already baptized candidates for the celebration of reconciliation. The rite states:

> Along with the candidates, their sponsors and the larger liturgical assembly also participate in the celebration of the penitential rite. Therefore the rite is adapted in such a way that it benefits all the participants. This penitential rite may also help to prepare the candidates to celebrate the sacrament of penance.[42]

Because this celebration may take place outside the context of the Sunday liturgy, the parish priest will do well to encourage the full participation of the community; clearly all will benefit.

The structure of the Penitential Rite (Scrutiny) is as follows:

Introductory Rites

- Greeting and Introduction
- Prayer

39. RCIA, 459.

40. RCIA, 462.

41. RCIA, 463.

42. RCIA, 461.

Liturgy of the Word

- Readings
- Homily
- Invitation to Silent Prayer
- Intercessions for the Candidates
- Prayer over the Candidates
- Dismissal of the Assembly (if occurring at a Liturgy of the Word)

Liturgy of the Eucharist

The rite's greeting underscores the reality that it "will have different meanings for the different participants," but that all "are going to hear the comforting message of pardon for sin, for which they will praise the Father's mercy."[43] The prayer designed for the rite (if celebrated on the Second Sunday of Lent, the Collect for that day may be used) beautifully acknowledges sin and the need for mercy as a part of our common lot:

> Lord of infinite compassion and steadfast love,
> your sons and daughters stand before you
> in humility and trust.
> Look with compassion on us
> as we acknowledge our sinfulness.
> Stretch out your hand
> to save us and raise us up.
> Do not allow the power of darkness
> to triumph over us,
> but keep us free from sin
> as members of Christ's body
> and sheep of your own flock.
>
> We ask this through our Lord Jesus Christ, your Son,
> who lives and reigns with you and the Holy Spirit,
> one God, for ever and ever.[44]

After the proclamation of the readings is the homily, in which the presider is to "prepare all those in the assembly for conversion and repentance and give the meaning of the penitential rite (scrutiny) in the light of the Lenten liturgy and of the spiritual

---

43. RCIA, 464.
44. RCIA, 465.

journey of the candidates."[45] The presider then invites the candidates to come forward with their sponsors, asking the candidates to either bow their heads or kneel down while the community as one prays in silence.

After a period of silence, all stand together and pray the intercessions for the candidates. These intercessions differ substantially from those used in the scrutinies for the elect, as they could be understood as applicable to all members of the community. For example: "That these candidates may come to a deeper appreciation of their baptism into Christ's death and resurrection"; "That they may grow to love and seek virtue and holiness of life"; "That they may share with others the joy they have found in their faith."[46] Surely the message of these intercessions pertains to each member of the assembly; we are all in need of continuing conversion. The prayer that closes the intercessions and is prayed over the candidates alludes to the Transfiguration (the Gospel on the Second Sunday of Lent), which presents a profound image for the life-situation of those seeking the fullness of life in the Church:

> Lord God,
> in the mystery of the transfiguration
> your Son revealed his glory to the disciples
> and prepared them for his death and resurrection.
>
> Open the minds and hearts of these candidates
> to the presence of Christ in their lives.
> May they humbly acknowledge their sins and failings
> and be freed of whatever obstacles and falsehoods
> keep them from adhering wholeheartedly to your kingdom.
>
> We ask this through Christ our Lord.[47]

At the end of this prayer, similar to the scrutiny rites, the presider lays hands on each of the candidates and, with hands outstretched over the candidates, concludes the rite with this prayer:

> Lord Jesus,
> you are the only-begotten Son,
> whose kingdom these candidates acknowledge

45. RCIA, 467.

46. RCIA, 469.

47. RCIA, 470.

> and whose glory they seek.
> Pour out upon them the power of your Spirit,
> that they may be fearless witnesses to your Gospel
> and one with us in the communion of love,
> for you are Lord for ever and ever.[48]

A song may be sung before the assembly is dismissed. If the penitential rite takes place during a Mass, the Liturgy of the Eucharist follows.

Candidates received into full communion of the Catholic Church are confirmed at the same liturgy.

The final rite to be celebrated with those who were baptized in a "separated ecclesial Community"[49] is the Reception of Baptized Christians into the Full Communion of the Catholic Church." The RCIA states: "The rite is so arranged that no greater burden than necessary (see Acts 15:28) is required for the establishment of communion and unity."[50] It is very important that this rite be celebrated without any sense of triumphalism. Again, the RCIA states:

> Any appearance of triumphalism should be carefully avoided and the manner of celebrating this Mass should be decided beforehand and with

48. RCIA, 470.
49. RCIA, 473.
50. RCIA, 473.

> a view to the particular circumstances. Both the ecumenical implications and the bond between the candidate and the parish community should be considered. Often it will be preferable to celebrate the Mass with only a few relatives and friends. If for a serious reason Mass cannot be celebrated, the reception should at least take place within a liturgy of the word, whenever this is possible. The person to be received into full communion should be consulted about the form of reception.[51]

While the Church recognizes that baptized non-Catholic Christians need to receive *catechumenal* instruction, "anything that would equate candidates for reception with those who are catechumens is to be absolutely avoided."[52] For example, for those seeking full communion, there is to be no "abjuration of heresy," but instead only the simple profession of faith.[53]

Unlike the elect who are to celebrate the sacraments of initiation at the Easter Vigil, there is no designated time for the celebration of reception into full communion. While many parishes have the custom of celebrating this rite within the Easter Vigil, the instruction to avoid any hint of triumphalism may suggest that this is the wrong setting for it. In fact, the *National Statutes for the Catechumenate* instructs that the Easter Vigil is not the appropriate time for reception:

> It is preferable that reception into full communion not take place at the Easter Vigil lest there be any confusion of such baptized Christians with the candidates for baptism, possible misunderstanding of or even reflection upon the sacrament of baptism celebrated in another Church or ecclesial community, or any perceived triumphalism in the liturgical welcome into the Catholic eucharistic community.[54]

Nevertheless, the RCIA offers a combined rite for the reception into full communion at the Easter Vigil.[55] Pastors must reflect carefully upon the ecclesial benefit of celebrating this rite at any point in the liturgical year "at the Sunday Eucharist of the parish community."[56] It seems far more appropriate to receive baptized Christians into full

51. RCIA, 475.
52. RCIA, 477.
53. RCIA, 479.
54. NS, 33.
55. RCIA, 34.
56. NS, 32.

communion with the Catholic Church at the point on their journey when they are ready.

The structure for the Rite of Reception is as follows:

Liturgy of the Word

- Readings
- Homily

Celebration of Reception

- Invitation
- Profession of Faith
- Act of Reception
- Confirmation
    - Laying On of Hands
    - Anointing with Chrism
- Celebrant's Sign of Welcome
- General Intercessions
- Sign of Peace

Liturgy of the Eucharist

When this celebration takes place within the context of the Sunday Mass, the Mass of that particular Sunday is to be celebrated; however, on other days, the Mass "For Christian Unity" may be used.[57] After the proclamation of the readings and the homily, in which the presider "should express gratitude to God for those being received and allude to their own baptism as the basis for their reception,"[58] he invites the one seeking full communion forward with his or her sponsor:

> N., of your own free will you have asked to be received into the full communion of the Catholic Church. You have made your decision after careful thought under the guidance of the Holy Spirit. I now invite you to come forward with your sponsor and in the presence of this community to profess the Catholic faith. In this faith you will be one with us for the first time at the eucharistic table of the Lord Jesus, the sign of the Church's unity.[59]

57. RCIA, 487.
58. RCIA, 489.
59. RCIA, 490.

The candidate proceeds to join the entire assembly in reciting the Nicene Creed. At the conclusion of the Creed, the candidate adds: "I believe and profess all that the holy Catholic Church believes, teaches, and proclaims to be revealed by God."[60] If Confirmation does not follow, the presider lays his right hand on the candidate's head and states the act of reception:

> N., the Lord receives you into the Catholic Church.
> His loving kindness has led you here,
> so that in the unity of the Holy Spirit
> you may have full communion with us
> in the faith that you have professed in the presence of his family.[61]

Canon Law (Canon 883 2°) gives the priest the faculty to confirm the Christian who has been received into the Church, and the *National Statutes for the Catechumenate* mandates that "the confirmation of such candidates for reception should not be deferred, nor should they be admitted to the eucharist until they are confirmed."[62] The *National Statutes* continues by suggesting that if the local bishop wishes to personally confirm those received into the Church, then he should be the one to receive them.[63] The celebration of Confirmation follows the pattern of that described in the Easter Vigil.

An interesting addition to the rite is that after the candidate is confirmed, the celebrant extends a sign of welcome. The RCIA states: "The celebrant then takes the hands of the newly received person into his own as a sign of friendship and acceptance."[64] Although the rite of Confirmation just celebrated contains the exchange of a greeting of peace, this gesture is intended to express hospitality and welcome. Again, while avoiding any sense of triumphalism, pastors ought to consider how the community might be invited to express a gesture of acceptance, whether that be through applause or the singing of an appropriate song. The celebration of reception nears completion with the general intercessions, in which the one received into full communion is mentioned.[65] A sign of

60. RCIA, 491.
61. RCIA, 492.
62. NS, 35.
63. NS, 35.
64. RCIA, 495.
65. RCIA, 496.

peace, understood as a greeting between the assembly and the candidate, serves as the actual conclusion of reception. This may seem redundant if the earlier sign of welcome includes some gesture of acceptance on the part of the entire community; thus, the Sign of Peace may occur at its usual place. The Liturgy of the Eucharist proceeds as usual, with the reception of the Eucharist for the first time on the part of the newly received, drawing the ritual action of reception to a final close.

Christian Initiation of Children Who Have Reached Catechetical Age

While having explored the issue of initiating adults who have already been baptized, a major component of Part II of the RCIA, "Rites for Particular Circumstances," Part II opens with a catechetical process for children who have reached the age of reason.[66] The RCIA states:

> This form of the rite of Christian initiation is intended for children, not baptized as infants, who have attained the use of reason and are of catechetical age. They seek Christian initiation either at the direction of their parents or guardians or, with parental permission, on their own

A number of factors need to be considered regarding the formation of children of catechetical age.

66. See *Code of Canon Law*, c. 852 §2.

> initiative. Such children are capable of receiving and nurturing a personal faith and of recognizing an obligation in conscience. But they cannot yet be treated as adults because, at this stage of their lives, they are dependent on their parents or guardians and are still strongly influenced by their companions and their social surroundings.[67]

Pastors, therefore, have a particular responsibility to ensure the proper formation for the unique circumstances of children of catechetical age who wish to be baptized and participate fully in the life of the Church. A number of factors need to be considered regarding the catechetical formation of these children, including their ages and whether their parents are also seeking initiation. The authors of the *Guide for Celebrating® Christian Initiation with Children* note that "at times it is appropriate and effective to combine catechumenal sessions for children and adults, and at other times, it is best for sessions to be separate."[68] "When children and parents from the same family are candidates for initiation, especially beneficial is a family-centered process in which parents and children journey together," the authors state.[69]

Nevertheless, the *National Statutes for the Catechumenate* maintains that the process of initiation for children of catechetical age should resemble the general pattern of the adult catechumenate with necessary age-related adaptations.[70] These children "receive the sacraments of baptism, confirmation, and eucharist at the Easter Vigil, together with the older catechumens."[71] Furthermore, not suggesting that unbaptized children of catechetical age be trained with the already baptized, the *National Statutes* offers the following recommendation:

> Some elements of the ordinary catechetical instruction of baptized children before their reception of the sacraments of confirmation and eucharist may be appropriately shared with catechumens of catechetical age. Their condition and status as catechumens, however, should not be compromised or confused, nor should they receive the sacraments of

67. RCIA, 252.

68. Rita Burns Senseman, Victoria M. Tufano, Paul Turner, and D. Todd Williamson, *Guide for Celebrating® Christian Initiation with Children* (Chicago: Liturgy Training Publications, 2017), 123.

69. *Guide for Celebrating Christian Initiation with Children*, p. 123.

70. NS, 18.

71. NS, 18.

> initiation in any sequence other than that determined in the ritual of Christian initiation.[72]

In other words, pastors are not permitted to separate the sacraments of initiation, one from another, in the case of unbaptized children of catechetical age, nor are they to receive Eucharist prior to Confirmation, as is the experience of many children baptized as infants.

The pastor needs to ensure the support of children seeking initiation. This is particularly true when children have reached the teenage years and are struggling to navigate a variety of passages in their lives, from establishing social groups, to balancing the demands of school and athletics, to going through changes in sexual development. To throw at teenagers the demands of following Christ and becoming his disciples is often overwhelming. The outcomes of many Confirmation programs witness to the challenge of making faith relevant to teens. The RCIA states that providing "companionship" is a fundamental component of catechizing children:

> The children's progress in the formation they receive depends on the help and example of their companions and on the influence of their parents. Both these factors should therefore be taken into account.
>
> 1. Since the children to be initiated often belong to a group of children of the same age who are already baptized and are preparing for confirmation and eucharist, their initiation progresses gradually and within the supportive setting of this group of companions.
>
> 2. It is to be hoped that the children will also receive as much help and example as possible from the parents, whose permission is required for the children to be initiated and to live the Christian life. The period of initiation will also provide a good opportunity for the family to have contact with priests and catechists.[73]

Companion here means a peer who takes part in the catechetical group and accompanies the catechumen in the rites. Thus, parish priests ought to work with both the children and their parents to guarantee that they have a suitable companion and are surrounded

72. NS, 19.

73. RCIA, 254.

by a nurturing and supportive family structure for their journey into the Christian faith.

The rite notes that children are to participate in the liturgical rites in a smaller setting.[74] However, the authors of *Guide to Celebrating® Christian Initiation with Children* explain that many parishes find that a celebration with adults and children is an effective adaptation. [75]

Marriage Issues

It is perhaps unfortunate that a book describing the blessed work of making Christian disciples ends with a brief discussion of the thorny dilemmas surrounding marriage issues and annulments. Nevertheless, it is here where the pastoral sensitivity of the pastor can be of tremendous value in the lives of men and women seeking to follow after Christ. Regarding the situation of "irregular marriages," Pope Francis writes in his 2016 postsynodal letter *Amoris laetitia*:

> A pastor cannot feel that it is enough simply to apply moral laws to those living in "irregular" situations, as if they were stones to throw at people's lives. This would bespeak the closed heart of one used to hiding behind the Church's teachings, "sitting on the chair of Moses and judging at times with superiority and superficiality difficult cases and wounded families. . . . Discernment must help to find possible ways of responding to God and growing in the midst of limits. By thinking that everything is black and white, we sometimes close off the way of grace and of growth, and discourage paths of sanctification which give glory to God. . . . The practical pastoral care of ministers and of communities must not fail to embrace this reality.[76]

Throughout his entire letter, Francis articulates the need for pastoral ministers to respond to situations of family crisis and marital irregularities with compassion and care. Very early on in the Christian initiation process, the priest ought to investigate the marriage status of inquirers. Upon the discovery of any problems, it becomes his responsibility to help couples regularize their marital

74. RCIA, 257.

75. *Guide for Celebrating Christian Initiation with Children*, 122.

76. *Amoris laetitia*, 305.

status. All of this is to be done to provide pastoral care and companionship along the faith journey.

Several basics of canon law that concern the Sacrament of Matrimony should be familiar to priests involved with the Christian initiation process. First, the Catholic Church presumes that most marriages, either civil or religious, are valid (canon 1060). Second, a marriage contracted with at least one Catholic falls under the purview of canon law (canon 1059). Third, marriages between two baptized Christians, even when neither party is Catholic, are considered sacramental marriages (canon 1055 §2). Fourth, a marriage that has been ratified and consummated cannot be dissolved (Canon 1141). Beyond these fundamentals, pastors are also expected to understand the validity (or invalidity) of marital bonds, which ought to be clearly spelled out by the diocesan tribunal.

The two primary marriage irregularities that priests will encounter when working with those who desire to be initiated or received into the Church involve convalidations and annulments. Convalidations seek to regularize marriages in which a Catholic party failed to fulfill the "form" of the Church. In these cases the marriage must be convalidated in order to be considered sacramental. For instance, perhaps the catechumen or the candidate seeking to be received into full communion is legally married to a Catholic, but the marriage was outside the Church. In this case, the marriage must be convalidated. The second irregularity, namely marriages requiring an annulment, is much more involved for the priest and the couple. Because annulments may take a considerable amount of time, it is important that the pastor investigate marital situations early on in the process. Pastors recount horror stories of not being able to celebrate the Easter sacraments with individuals whose marriages had not yet been annulled. Once again, the local tribunal functions to help priests guide couples through the annulment process.

The Church demands that, except in danger of death, candidates who are in invalid marriages cannot be received into full communion or sacramentally initiated until the marriage is validated. This does not mean that men and women in irregular marriages should be prevented from entering the process; they may be welcomed in the Rite of Acceptance and enter the Order of

Catechumens. However, the pastor should explain to those in this situation that they may have to wait longer than normal for the celebration of the Easter sacraments and full communion. In fact, the best pastoral practice on the part of the minister is to make clear that there is no guarantee that the tribunal will nullify a former marriage. In a similar vein, when one or both parties of an engaged couple is participating in the Christian initiation process, pastors should counsel them to plan the marriage for after the completion of initiation.

In the end, the priest is challenged to present the marriage law of the Church, often critiqued as being burdensome, as containing a beautiful wisdom regarding the gift of unity and the manifestation of divine communion. The pastor must approach his role as a caring counselor. In a very real way, the pastor "stirs up" the Church's mercy and helps those in problematic marriage situations to experience freedom and new life; he guides those to the waters of life where they may find healing and wholeness and hope in the fullness of Christ.

Resources

Anslinger, Leisa, Martin F. Connell, Mary A. Ehle, Biagio Mazza, and Victoria M. Tufano. *The Living Word™: Leading RCIA Dismissals, Year B*. Chicago: Liturgy Training Publications, Fall 2017. The step-by-step format this resource provides will instill confidence in catechists as they facilitate discussion on the Sunday readings, Separate dismissal resources will be offered for Years A, B, and C.

Birmingham, Mary. *Year-Round Catechumenate*. Chicago: Liturgy Training Publications, 2003. Mary Birmingham encourages readers to rethink the common model of a Christian initiation process based on the school year. Since the process of initiation exists at the heart of the Church's life, she argues that it should be on the same schedule as the Church. Guiding readers step-by-step through the periods and rites of the Christian initiation process, Birmingham offers pastors, initiation teams, and liturgy committees all the resources needed to imagine, understand, and implement a year-round catechumenate.

Clay, Michael. *A Harvest for God: Christian Initiation in the Rural and Small-Town Parish*. Chicago: Liturgy Training Publications, 2003. Christian initiation teams in rural areas and small towns will find this book considers initiation in a way that is appropriate to the situation and culture of the parish. Any parish with a limited number of people and resources will find *A Harvest for God* useful.

Connors, Michael, csc. *Strengthening Parish Discipleship: Preaching with the Rites and Seasons of Christian Initiation*. Chicago: Liturgy Training Publications, Fall 2017. Father Connors assists homilists with communicating the vision of Christian initiation to the assembly.

Eschenauer, Donna M. *The Role of the Coordinator in Christian Initiation: A Pastoral and Practical Guide*. Chicago: Liturgy Training Publications, 2017. While providing the vision of Christian initiation, this resource outlines the role of the coordinator in animating the parish and forming the team.

Galipeau, Jerry. *Apprenticed to Christ: Activities for Practicing the Catholic Way of Life*. Franklin Park, IL: World Library Publications, 2007. This book suggests ways those in the process of initiation can be integrated into the life of the parish, making use of the various ministries, outreaches, and activities already established in the parish. This collection of activities is rooted in paragraph 75 of the RCIA, and is geared toward the Sundays of the liturgical year.

Galipeau, Jerry, editor. *The Impact of the RCIA: Stories, Reflections, Challenges*. Chicago: World Library Publications, 2008. A wealth of articles provide firsthand accounts on Christian initiation from many aspects—global, liturgical, catechetical, musical, Hispanic, African American, rural, urban, Episcopal, and ecumenical.

Gensler, Gael, OSF, Timothy A. Johnston, Corinna Laughlin, and Kyle Lechtenberg. *Disciples Making Disciples / Discípulos haciendo discípulos*. Chicago: Liturgy Training Publications, Fall 2017. Through bulletin inserts, this digital resource provides parishes a way to form both English- and Spanish-speaking members of the assembly on their responsibilities in the Christian initiation process.

Huck, Gabe. *The Three Days: Parish Prayer in the Paschal Triduum*. Revised edition. Chicago: Liturgy Training Publications, 1992. This is a thorough exploration of all the moments that make up the great Paschal Triduum. It gives a solid theology and spirituality of the whole three-day feast as it can be lived out in a parish setting. This approach provides a solid context for the parish's initiation ministry to see and understand its place in the observance of these most holy days.

Huels, John. *The Catechumenate and the Law: A Pastoral and Canonical Commentary for the Church in the United States*. Chicago: Liturgy training Publications, 2003. As a rite of the Church, the RCIA is a canonical document as well as a liturgical one. This eminent canonist examines how the law affects persons (candidates, catechumens, ministers, children, sponsors, and godparents) and situations (invalid or doubtful Baptism and Confirmations, marriage cases, delaying Confirmation, and record keeping), offering pastoral and canonical guidance.

Hughes, Kathleen. *Saying Amen: A Mystagogy of Sacrament*. Chicago: Liturgy Training Publications, 1999. The author shoes how our experience of the sacraments opens the doors to God's transformative power, through Christ and in the Spirit. This book gives a wonderfully accessible approach to seeing how, as Catholics, we really are called to live a sacramental life.

Kavanagh, Aidan. *The Shape of Baptism: The Rite of Christian Initiation*. Collegeville, MN: Pueblo Publishing Company, Inc., 1978. While Kavanagh offers an analysis of Roman initiatory tradition in this book, the commentary also is a pastoral one.

Lewinski, Ron. *An Itroduction to the RCIA: The Vision of Christian Initiation*. Chicago: Liturgy Training Publications, Fall 2017. This resource serves as a primer for those involved in Christian initiation ministry. It offers an overview of the four periods of Christian initiation and their accompanying rituals. Questions are provided for discussion and reflection.

McMahon, J. Michael. *The Rite of Christian Initiation of Adults: A Pastoral Liturgical Commentary*. Revised edition. Washington, DC: Federation of Diocesan Liturgical Commissions, 2002. This study guide presents documentation from the *Rite of Christian Initiation of Adults* and other pertinent Church documents, commentary, and study questions for every aspect of the initiation of adults.

Morris, Thomas H. *The RCIA: Transforming the Church: A Resource for Pastoral Implementation*. Revised and updated edition. New York: Paulist Press, 1997. If every RCIA minister is to have the *Rite of Christian Initiation of Adults* in one hand, then having Morris' book in the other hand will round it all out. This book is an excellent resource that takes the vision of the RCIA and shows *how* that vision can take shape in the parish setting.

Paprocki, Joe, and D. Todd Williamson. *Great Is the Mystery: The Formational Power of Liturgy*. Chicago: Liturgy Training Publications, 2012. Catechesis and liturgy are connected in this book that walks readers through the foundational principles of a Catholic liturgical life. The authors, experts in the field, break open the principles, making them accessible and understandable. They also explore the various elements and dynamics of a liturgical spirituality and give an in-depth look at each part of the weekly celebration of the parish Eucharist.

Ruzicki, Michael. *Guide for Training Initiation Ministers: An Introduction to the RCIA*. Chicago: Liturgy Training Publications, 2017. This resource provides Christian initiation coordinators with the tools they need to form all involved with the parish initiation ministry. Complete with outlines and videos, this resource is designed to be used with *An Introduction to the RCIA: The Vision of Christian Initiation*, by Ronald Lewiniski.

Searle, Mark. "The Journey of Conversion." *Worship* 54:1 (1980): 35–55. This essay is particularly helpful in portraying conversion as a process that is similar to a rite of passage. Searle contends that every conversion experience is rooted in a crisis that calls for surrendering to the truth of one's life.

Senseman, Rita Burns. *Guide to Adapting the RCIA for Children*. Chicago: Liturgy Training Publications, Fall 2017. From her experience as a catechist, the author guides directors of religious education, catechists, and coordinators of Christian initiation in adapting rites appropriately for children. At the same time, she stays faithful to the vision of the rite.

Senseman, Rita Burns, Victoria M. Tufano, Paul Turner, and D. Todd Williamson. *Guide to Celebrating® the Rite of Christian Initiation of Adults with Children*. Chicago: Liturgy Training Publications, 2017. The authors consider the adaptations made for children in Part II of the *Rite of Christian Initiation of Adults* as well as the appropriateness of including children with adults in the rites. The book also provides guidance for receiving children into full communion with the Catholic Church.

Stice, Randy. *Understanding the Sacraments of Initiation: A Rite-Based Approach*. Chicago: Liturgy Training Publications, 2017. Not only does the resource guide readers through the rites of Baptism, Confirmation, and Eucharist, but explores the liturgical history, sacramental theology, and Old Testament foundations of each rite.

Tudela, Michaela, with contributions from Rita Burns Senseman and the editors at Liturgy Training Publications. Edited by Victoria M. Tufano. *Guide to the RCIA for Children: Q&A for Parents*. Chicago: Liturgy Training Publications, Fall 2017. This informational supplement to the *Guide to Adapting the RCIA for Children* (and the resource for teens) will help parents and guardians of children seeking to become Catholic. It contains frequently asked questions and answers. This small resource may be given to parents after the initial meeting with the coordinator of Christian initiation or director of religious education.

Tufano, Victoria M., editor. *Celebrating the Rites of Adult Initiation: Pastoral Reflections*. Chicago: Liturgy Training Publications, 1992. This collection of essays offers the insights of Kathleen Hughes, J. Michael Joncas, Rita Ferrone, James Moudry, Catherine Mowry Lacugna, Mark Francis, Marguerite Main, Ronald Oakham, and Edward Foley on the rites of initiation. These essays look at the scrutinies, the rite of acceptance, and the presentations. Also included are commentaries on the Minor Exorcisms, the taking of a new name, and the Liturgy of the Word.

Tufano, Victoria M. *Disciples Making Disciples: The Role of the Assembly in Christian Initiation*. Chicago: Liturgy Training Publications, 2017. This booklet helps parishioners understand their role in the initiation process. Available in English and Spanish.

Tufano, Victoria M., Paul Turner, and D. Todd Williamson. *Guide for Celebrating® Christian Initiation with Adults*. Chicago: Liturgy Training Publications, 2017. After exploring the theological and historical developments of Christian initiation, the authors guide the readers through the celebration of the rites during each period and step of the *Rite of Christian Initiation of Adults*. The resource provides additional materials on the initiation process and answers queries about the RCIA.

Tuner, Paul. *The Hallelujah Highway: A History of the Catechumenate.* Chicago: Liturgy Training Publications, 2000. Turner's rich narrative recounts the history of the catechumenate through stories of the people and documents that shaped the rites of initiation from the earliest days of the Church to the present.

Turner, Paul. *When Other Christians Become Catholic.* Collegeville, MN: The Liturgical Press, 2007. The author presents historical and ecumenical contexts in which to understand what we do when we receive baptized Christians into the full communion of the Catholic Church. He challenges us to examine our practices to reflect the true nature of what we are doing when we receive other Christians into the Catholic Church and in this way to witness to the unity of Christians as it is now and as it is to be.

Wagner, Nick. *The Way of Faith: A Field Guide for the RCIA Process.* Twenty-Third Publications, 2008. Readers will find a solid overview of the process of initiation as it can be implemented in the parish setting. Wagner does an excellent job of addressing each of the periods of the initiation process, including the who, what, where, when, why, and how of each period.

Whitaker, E. C. *Documents of the Baptismal Liturgy.* London: SPCK, 1960. This resource contains the ancient baptismal liturgies upon which the contemporary RCIA has its foundation.

Yarnold, Edward. *The Awe-Inspiring Rites of Initiation: The Origins of the RCIA.* Second Edition, Collegeville, MN: Liturgical Press, 1994. *The Awe-Inspiring Rites of Initiation* first came out in 1972 but was recast two decades later to correspond with the *Rite of Christian Initiation of Adults.* In this book, students of liturgy and catechists will gain a better understanding of the RCIA as they learn about the catechumenal practices of the fourth century and read sermons on the sacraments preached by Cyril, Ambrose, Chrysostom, and Theodore. Through these sermons, the Church Fathers guided neophytes to contemplate the Christian mysteries.

Out-of-Print Resources

Joncas, Jan Michael. *Forum Essays*. No. 4, *Preaching the Rites of Christian Initiation*. Chicago: Liturgy Training Publications, 1994. In the four essays in this volume, Joncas defines liturgical preaching, outlines the forms liturgical preaching may take in the rites of Christian initiation, gives a process for preparing liturgical preaching, and provides models of such preaching.

Madigan, Shawn. *Forum Essays*. No. 5, *Liturgical Spirituality and the Rite of Christian Initiation of Adults*. Chicago: Liturgy Training Publications, 1997. The five essays in this volume consider the rites of Christian initiation as formative and expressive of a liturgical spirituality.

Mitchell, Nathan D. *Forum Essays*. No. 2, *Eucharist as Sacrament of Initiation*. Chicago: Liturgy Training Publications, 2003. Within three essays, Nathan Mitchell considers the meaning of the neophyte's participation in the paschal meal.

Oakham, Ron A., editor. *One at the Table: The Reception of Baptized Christians*. Chicago: Liturgy Training Publications, 1995. This book begins with five articles offering theological foundations for understanding the issues surrounding the reception of the baptized. Oakham then presents a pastoral plan for ministering to the baptized person seeking reception into the full communion of the Catholic Church.

Sieverding, Dale J. *Forum Essays*. No. 7, *The Reception of Baptized Christians: A History and Evaluation*. Chicago: Liturgy Training Publications, 2001. The essays examine the history of the reception of baptized Christians, from the patristic period through the post-conciliar development of the ritual.

Vincie, Catherine. *Forum Essays*. No. 1, *The Role of the Assembly in Christian Initiation*. Chicago: Liturgy Training Publications, 1993. The essays in this volume consider the responsibility that the order of initiation expects of the assembly.

Glossary

Adult For the purpose of sacramental initiation, a person who reaches the age of reason (also called the age of discretion or catechetical age), usually regarded to be seven years of age, is an adult. A person who has reached that age is to be initiated into the Church according to the Rite of Christian Initiation of Adults and receive the three sacraments of initiation together, although the catechesis should be adapted to the individual's needs. Before this age, the person is considered an infant and is baptized using the Rite of Baptism for Children.

Apostles' Creed The ancient baptismal statement of the Church's faith. The questions used in the celebration of Baptism correspond to the statements of the Apostles' Creed.

Baptismal font The pool or basin at which the Sacrament of Baptism is administered.

Blessing Any prayer that praises and thanks God. In particular, blessing describes those prayers in which God is praised because of some person or object, and thus the individual or object is seen to have become specially dedicated or sanctified because of the prayer of faith.

Book of the Elect A book into which the names of those catechumens who have been chosen, or elected, for initiation at the next Easter Vigil, are written at or before the Rite of Election.

Book of the Gospels A ritual book from which the passages from the accounts of the Gospel prescribed for Masses on Sundays, solemnities, feasts of the Lord and of the saints, and ritual Masses are proclaimed; also called an evangeliary.

Candidate In its broadest definition, the term refers to anyone preparing to receive a sacrament. In the *Rite of Christian Initiation of Adults*, the term is used as a general designation for adults who are expressing an interest in the Catholic faith, whether baptized or not. In common usage, candidate is used for a baptized person preparing for reception into the full communion of the Catholic Church; an unbaptized person inquiring about preparing for Christian initiation is called an inquirer.

Catechesis Instruction and spiritual formation in the faith, teachings, and traditions of the Church.

Catechetical age Usually considered to be seven years of age; also called the age of reason or the age of discretion. For the purpose of Christian initiation, a person who has reached catechetical age is considered an adult and is to be initiated into the Church according to the *Rite of Christian Initiation of Adults.*

Catechumen An unbaptized person who has declared his or her intention to prepare for the sacraments of initiation and has been accepted into the Order of Catechumens. Catechumens, though not yet fully initiated, are joined to the Church and are considered part of the household of Christ.

Catechumenate The second of four periods in the process of Christian initiation as described in the *Rite of Christian Initiation of Adults.* The period begins with the Rite of Acceptance into the Order of Catechumens. It is a period of nurturing and growth of the catechumens' faith and conversion to God in Christ. Sometimes the term catechumenate is used to refer to the entire initiation process.

Celebrant The presiding minister at worship.

Child For the purposes of Christian initiation, one who has not yet reached the age of discernment (age of reason, presumed to be seven years of age) and therefore cannot profess personal faith.

Chrism One of the three holy oils. It is consecrated by the bishop at the Chrism Mass and used at the Baptism of infants, at Confirmation, at the ordination of priests and bishops, and at the dedication of churches and altars. Chrism is scented, usually with balsam.

Companion In the Christian initiation process with children of catechetical age, a baptized child of an age similar to the child catechumen who takes part in the catechetical group and accompanies the catechumen in the rites.

Confirmation The sacrament that continues the initiation process begun in Baptism and marks the sealing of the Holy Spirit. It is administered through an anointing with Christ on the forehead with the words, "N., be sealed with the Gift of the Holy Spirit," preceded by the imposition of hands.

Dismissal The final, formal invitation by the deacon or, in his absence, the priest for the assembly to go forth from the liturgical celebration. The word can also refer to the dismissal of the catechumens after the homily at Mass.

Easter Vigil The liturgy celebrated during the night before Easter Sunday; it begins after nightfall and ends before daybreak on Sunday. It includes the Baptism, Confirmation, and reception of the Eucharist of the elect. All present renew their baptismal promises.

Elect Catechumens who have been formally called, or elected, by the Church for Baptism, Confirmation, and Eucharist at the next Easter Vigil.

Ephphetha Rite A rite of opening the ears and the mouth, associated with the celebration of Baptism. The rite, which has its origin in Mark 7:31–37, Jesus' healing of a deaf man, prays that the one being baptized may hear and profess the faith. It may be performed with the elect as part of their preparation on Holy Saturday for initiation at the Easter Vigil or as part of the Rite of Baptism for Children.

Exorcism A prayer or command given to cast out the presence of the devil. The Rite of Baptism for Children contains a prayer of exorcism; the *Rite of Christian Initiation of Adults* contains prayers of exorcism as part of the rites belonging to the Period of the Catechumenate and as part of the scrutinies. There is a Rite of Exorcism for use in the case of possession; it may be used only with the express permission of a bishop and only by mandated priest-exorcists.

Evangelization The continuing mission of the Church to spread the Gospel of Jesus Christ to all people. Evangelization is done during the precatechumenate, which involves the invitation, the welcoming, the witness, the sharing of faith, and the proclamation of the Gospel to inquirers.

Faculty A right granted to enable a person to do something, usually referring to a right granted to a priest or deacon by law or by the bishop.

Godparents Members of the Christian community, chosen for their good example and their close relationship to the one being baptized, who are present at the celebration of Baptism and provide guidance and assistance to the one baptized afterward.

Holy Saturday The Saturday within the Sacred Paschal Triduum. It is a day marked by meditation, prayer, and fasting in anticipation of the Resurrection of the Lord. Several Preparation Rites for the elect who will be receiving the sacraments of initiation at the Vigil are proper to this day.

Immersion A method of Baptism in which the candidate is submerged either entirely or partially in the baptismal water.

Infusion A method of Baptism in which the baptismal water is poured over the head of the candidate.

Inquirer An unbaptized adult who is in the very first stage of the process of Christian initiation.

Inquiry Another name given to the period of evangelization and precatechumenate, the first period or stage in the process of Christian initiation.

Initiation The process by which a person enters the faith life of the Church—from the catechumenate through the normally continuous celebration of the entrance rites of Baptism, Confirmation, and the Eucharist.

Laying On of Hands A gesture of blessing or invocation recorded in the New Testament in conjunction with prayer (for example, Acts 13:3; 2 Timothy 1:6). The gesture is performed by extending both hands forward with the palms turned downward. Depending on the circumstances, the hands may be placed on the person's head or stretched out over a group of people or over an object.

Litany of the Saints A litany that calls upon the saints to pray for the Church, believed to be the most ancient litany in the Church's worship.

Minor Rites Rites during the catechumenate, which include the Rite of Exorcism, Rite of Blessing, and Rite of Anointing.

Mystagogy The postbaptismal catechesis given to the newly baptized during Easter Time, wherein the neophyte and the local Church share the meaning of the initiatory mysteries and experience.

National Statutes for the Catechumenate A document issued by the Catholic bishops of the United States in 1986, and confirmed by the Apostolic See in 1988, constituting particular law for the implementation of the RCIA in the United States.

Neophyte One who is recently initiated. It comes from the word meaning new plant or twig, a new sprout on a branch. After the Period of Mystagogy the new Catholic is no longer called neophyte.

Oil of Catechumens The oil, blessed by the bishop at the Chrism Mass (or for pastoral reasons by the priest before the anointing) to be used in the anointing of the catechumens during the process of initiation.

Order of Catechumens The group to which an unbaptized adult who is preparing to receive the sacraments of initiation belongs after celebrating the Rite of Acceptance into the Order of Catechumens.

Paschal Mystery The saving mystery of Christ's Passion, Death, and Resurrection. It is the mystery that is celebrated and made present in every liturgy, and the mystery that every Christian is to imitate and be united with in everyday life.

Penance The sacrament by which the baptized, through the mercy of God, receive pardon for their sins and reconciliation with the Church. This sacrament is most commonly celebrated by the private confession of sin and expression of sorrow by a penitent to a confessor, who then offers absolution. It is also commonly called confession or the Sacrament of Reconciliation.

Postbaptismal catechesis Mystagogical catechesis, instruction given to the newly baptized, or neophytes, to help them deepen their understanding of the faith primarily through reflection on the sacraments they celebrated at Easter.

Precatechumenate A period of indeterminate length that precedes acceptance into the Order of Catechumens. In the Rite of Christian Initiation of Adults, this time is called the Period of Evangelization and Precatechumenate; it is also sometimes referred to as inquiry.

Preparation Rites Various rites that can be celebrated with the elect on Holy Saturday in proximate preparation for the celebration of the sacraments of initiation at the Easter Vigil that evening.

Presentations Rites whereby the Church entrusts the Creed and the Lord's Prayer, the ancient texts that express the hearts of the Church's faith, to the elect.

Propers Those texts in the Mass and in the Liturgy of the Hours that are particular to a given day.

Purification and Enlightenment The final period of the catechumenal process for unbaptized adults preparing for initiation in the Catholic Church. It is a time of intense spiritual preparation marked by the celebration of the scrutinies and the presentations. It usually coincides with Lent.

RCIA *Rite of Christian Initiation of Adults*, the official rite of the Roman Catholic Church for initiation of children of catechetical age and adults and the reception of baptized candidates.

Reception of Baptized Christians into the Full Communion of the Catholic Church The liturgical rite for receiving into the full communion of the Catholic Church an adult who was validly baptized in a non-Catholic Christian community.

Register of Catechumens The book in which the names of those unbaptized adults who have been accepted as catechumens is recorded. The names of the sponsors and the minister and the date and place of the celebration of the Rite of Acceptance into the Order of Catechumens should also be recorded. Each parish should have a Register of Catechumens.

Renunciation of Sin The ritual questioning that precedes the Profession of Faith made at Baptism or in the renewal of Baptism. There are two alternate forms of the formula for the renunciation of sin, each of which consists of three questions that center on the rejection of Satan and his works.

Rite of Baptism for Children The ritual book that gives the rites for the Baptism of children who have not yet attained the age of discretion (the age of reason), presumed to be about age seven.

***Rite of Christian Initiation of Adults* (RCIA)** The ritual book, part of the Roman Ritual, that gives the norms, directives, and ritual celebrations for initiating unbaptized adults and children who have reached catechetical age into Christ and incorporating them into the Church. The RCIA prescribes a sequence of periods and rites by which candidates transition from one stage to another, which culminate in the celebration of the sacraments of initiation, usually at the Easter Vigil.

Rite of Election The second step for unbaptized adults preparing for the sacraments of initiation, also called the Enrollment of Names. The rite closes the period of the catechumenate and marks the beginning of the Period of Purification and Enlightenment, which usually corresponds to Lent. With this rite the Church makes its election, or choice, of the catechumens to receive the sacraments. The Rite of Election normally takes place on or near the First Sunday of Lent.

Sacraments of Christian initiation The Sacraments of Baptism, Confirmation, and Eucharist. All three sacraments are necessary to be fully initiated into the Church. Adults, including children of catechetical age, receive the three sacraments in one liturgy when being initiated into the Church.

Sacred Paschal Triduum The three-day celebration of the Paschal Mystery of Christ that is the high point and center of the entire liturgical year. The Paschal Triduum begins with the Evening Mass of the Lord's Supper on Holy Thursday, solemnly remembers Christ's Death on Good Friday, reaches its zenith at the Easter Vigil with the Baptism of the elect into the mystery of Christ's Death and Resurrection, and concludes with Evening Prayer on Easter Sunday.

Scrutiny One of the three rites celebrated with the elect. It is a rite of self-searching and repentance intended to heal whatever is weak or sinful in the hearts of the elect, and to strengthen all that is good, in preparation for their reception of the Easter sacraments. The scrutinies are exorcisms by which the elect are delivered from the power of Satan and protected against temptation.

Sending of the Catechumens for Election An optional rite that may be celebrated before the catechumens take part in the Rite of Election. The rite, which usually takes place at Mass, expresses the parish community's approval and support of the catechumens' election by the bishop.

Sponsor In the Christian initiation of adults, one who accompanies a person seeking admission as a catechumen. The sponsor is someone who knows the candidate and is able to witness to the candidate's moral character, faith, and intention. He or she accompanies the candidate at the Rite of Acceptance into the Order of Catechumens and continues to accompany and support the person through the Period of the Catechumenate. In the celebration of the Sacrament of Confirmation with those who were baptized in infancy, the sponsor presents a person being confirmed to the minister of the sacrament. After the celebration of the sacrament, the sponsor helps the individual live in accord with their baptismal promises.

White garment The clothing, often similar to an alb, which is given to someone immediately after Baptism. This garment is a sign that the newly baptized person has put on new life in Christ. It is used in the Baptism of both adults and children.

Index